ROYAL LODGE, WINDSOR

Helen Cathcart

SAPERE BOOKS

ROYAL LODGE,
WINDSOR

Published by Sapere Books.

20 Windermere Drive, Leeds, England, LS17 7UZ,
United Kingdom

saperebooks.com

ISBN: 978-1-80055-459-7.

TABLE OF CONTENTS

1: THE NEW OCCUPANTS

I

Royal Lodge, Windsor, was the private country home of the late Queen Elizabeth the Queen Mother. For nearly twenty years it enshrined the happiness of her married life with King George VI, and it was thus the family home of both the present Queen Elizabeth II and her sister, Princess Margaret. Though by no means the largest, it is perhaps the best known of a score of grace-and-favour residences in Windsor Great Park. Twice in royal history it has provided a principal background as the chief home of the Sovereign, first for a time for George IV and then for George VI and, in the very different atmosphere of both these reigns, its discreet function as the domestic sanctuary of the monarch was continuously deprecated, soft-pedalled and masked by conventional reticence.

Royal Lodge is, in fact, one of a scattered group of dwellings, mansions, forts and follies in the southern recesses and environs of Windsor Great Park which have served royal pleasures and private needs ever since the carefree Charles II capered "all maudlin and kissing" with a drunken company at Cranbourne Tower. It has been the home of artists and courtiers and farmers and foresters, the picnic pavilion of queens and the lodging of young princes. It is linked with names as timeless as Marlborough and Nelson, John Nash and Walter Scott. Sir Robert Peel suggested it to Queen Victoria as an alternative to Osborne, and it was offered by Queen Victoria to her eldest son as a substitute for Sandringham. Twice, at least, the building on the site was demolished; until the last Georgian remnant was preserved by the determined and active though unlikely intervention of none other than the Prince Consort. There is a touch of strangeness in the thought that, three royal generations later, the Lodge should have become the home of a prince named after him, and the childhood home of a princess destined to follow Victoria as the next Queen Regnant.

For nearly a century, throughout the Victorian era and for thirty years afterwards, the Royal Lodge slipped from public awareness and was all but forgotten. Then, late in the nineteen twenties, a small, secluded, rather shabby house, it became the home of King George V's racing manager, Major Frederick Fetherstonhaugh, and accordingly a focus of racing gossip whenever the King was at Windsor. While her husband discussed his horses, Queen Mary conscientiously made a point of inspecting Mrs. Fetherstonhaugh's rose garden and aviary ... to the fretting dismay of her hostess, who would far rather have joined in the men's talk of bloodstock. When Major Fetherstonhaugh died, his widow indeed quickly decided to move to Norfolk and undertake the management of the Royal Stud at Sandringham. And at this point, in July and August, 1931, a brilliant new era dawned over the empty Lodge for, at the Balmoral dinner table, the Duke and Duchess of York seized the golden opportunity to mention themselves as potential new occupants.

The young couple, indeed, the future King George VI and his consort Queen Elizabeth, interrupted their summer holiday and returned to London, so eager were they not to miss their chance of the house. At the back of their minds, no doubt, was the worrying thought that some official of the Commissioners of Crown Lands might submit the name of a prospective tenant whom the King would find it difficult to refuse. In the records of the early thirties, one can sense the flurry of danger and a haste to make an inspection, as if a pair of inexperienced young house-hunters had been warned by an estate agent that other viewers were interested.

It made no difference that the house-hunters were the most popular couple in Britain. They unexpectedly hurried south from a Scottish castle to a shuttered and dust-sheeted Piccadilly mansion that could be only partly opened up for their stay of a night or two. They set out from a mansion in search of a cottage, but with such glowing hope and anxiety that the early September morning became burnished for ever afterwards as one of the decisive and special days of a lifetime.

If recollections are reliable, they drove in the Duke's Aster sports saloon which so often waited at the garden gate at the back of 145 Piccadilly. At this exit they could escape unseen into the park, in preference to the front cobbled forecourt of their London home; where every movement attracted public attention. They drove westward from London through the tram-clogged suburbs of Hammersmith and Chiswick and along the new wing of the Great West Road, past the dentrifice factories, past the new estates of semi-detached £495 houses and the signboards that proclaimed easy repayments and low deposits. They drove through a perimeter landscape where forlorn eighteenth-century inns on their last leases were flanked by abandoned orchards and decaying barns, past flat and unpeopled cabbage fields where was heard as yet no whisper of London Airport.

It was a rural scene in the desolate throes of transition to urban subtopia; and the travellers necessarily raced ahead in imagination, seeking relief to the spirit amid the glades of Windsor Great Park. The Duke and Duchess knew every inch of the road, chiefly from visits to Fort Belvedere, and yet that day's journey was spiced by adventure, the excitement of an impending decision that might bring an incalculable train of future events. No one recognised the young couple, save for the casual glance now and then, congealing to an astonished intent stare, that has become the modern homage of royalty in our time.

The little Duchess, petite and blue-eyed, still could not meet that startled, mesmerised gape without almost irrepressible amusement. Eight years of marriage had still not effaced her sense of ludicrous unreality. Her husband was less susceptible and less readily identified. His photograph in pallid monochrome seldom suggested to newspaper readers the taut, suntanned good looks of the youngish man at the wheel. Besides, the celebrity of King George V's second son was a pale glimmer of the incandescent adulation and public attention constantly focused on his elder brother, the Prince of Wales. The Duke of York had reached his thirty-sixth year tempered by training and inclination to his secondary role; and was modestly, incredulously unaware of the affection that his own example of domestic happiness had won from the nation.

So they came to the bridge across the Thames at Staines, more delectable with country air then than now. So to Staines, as Pepys said, "and got a guide who lost his way in the forest, till by help of the moone (which recompenses me for all the pains I ever took about studying of her motions) I led my guide into the way back again; and so we made a man rise that kept a gate, and so he carried us to Cranbourne. Where in the dark I perceive an old house new building with a great deal of rubbish, and was fain to go up a ladder to Sir G. Carteret's chamber. And there in his bed I sat down, and told him all my bad news, which troubled him mightily; but yet we were very merry, and made the best of it; and being myself weary did take leave… I to bed in my Lady's chamber that she uses to lie in, and where the Duchesse of York, that now is, was born. So to sleep…" But our story opens in 1931, not 1665, and in another part of the forest another Duchess of York comes to another gate of Windsor Great Park.

II

Bishops Gate, so named after a thirteenth-century family, is one of the least frequented, most concealed and less observed of all the ten main gates within the fourteen-mile fence of Windsor Great Park. It lies on the eastern verge, where the winding lanes of Egham and Runnymede and Englefield Green all confuse the stranger, and the inquirer might be as lost as Pepys but for signposts or friendly guidance in the well-fenced, well-shrubbed maze of residential roads. Fringed by bulky Edwardian and late Victorian houses, one such avenue can be passed without realising that it leads only to the park. It turns out indeed to be nearly a cul-de-sac, ending in a white-painted kissing-gate for walkers and a white gate for cars, guarded by a porter in soft green Windsor livery. Only the mellow brick and pleasing facade of a nearby house, unkempt perhaps yet unmistakably Georgian in its handsome entrance porch and fanlight, reinstates the tangible atmosphere of history.

The gatekeeper recognised the Duke of York's Aster and the gate was open almost before the car could slow down. Within the park, a glade of scattered oaks lay across the saucer of a shallow valley; and beyond the slate-roofed entrance cottages the green woodland of the private domain of Royal Lodge spread a curtain across the rising ground and filled the view.

This was the aspect that the Duchess — the late Queen Elizabeth the Queen Mother — was to come to know so well, seldom to see without a lifting of the heart and a sense of calm, of coming home. In 1931 she was already familiar with it, from sociable visits to the Fetherstonhaughs. It was once said that despite their age differences, Mrs. Fetherstonhaugh and the little Duchess were among the few women who could probe the crusty intolerance of old King George V and persuade him that all was not ill in the short skirts, shingled hair and cocktails of that time. There had been pleasant little parties at the Lodge when the Duchess had peeped from the windows and admired the situation of the house, never dreaming that it could one day be hers. Of all the grace-and-favour properties, none attracted her more, at least in the setting if not the house itself. But it was strange, inevitably, when the pleasant woman at the private entrance lodge opened the gate, and bobbed politely, and the newcomers knew that the welcoming smiles of the Fetherstonhaughs would not be awaiting them a mile farther on.

The entrance drive already flaunted the dandelions of more than a month of summer neglect. Nearer the house, in those days, it was apt to seem over-shielded by laurels and other dark, shiny shrubs. On the left the car passed the tiny ivy-hung mid-Victorian Chapel of All Saints, with its Gothic porch and belfry pinnacle, and then they swung past a daisy-covered lawn to the gravelled forecourt, walled within yew hedges, where the inner precinct of Royal Lodge began.

Two gentlemen from the Crown Estate office formed the welcoming party. Looking at the house with a newly exact and critical eye, the Duchess of York saw a two-storeyed box coated with greyish stucco, stained here and there with mossy damp and decay. Plaster finials decorated the parapet of the flat-topped roof as on some obscure provincial railway station, and chimneys rose everywhere in awkward profusion. An unhappy single-storeyed extension had been built against the frontage at some time and, to reach the front door, the newcomers had to traverse a long glass greenhouse. One of the Estate officials paced it out to show that this conservatory measured thirty-three yards by sixteen: space enough, he agreed, for a fine new wing. And then, opening a massive door in the cramped and narrow entrance hall, the explorers found themselves facing the coiling painted pipes and brass taps of a bathroom, and when their guide opened another door it was inadvertently to usher them into the mahogany-seated privacy of one of the smallest rooms of the establishment.

The story no doubt gained sparkle over the dinner table, and the Duchess's bubbling laughter and enthusiasm rang out as her guides ushered her more accurately through the other apartments. As Sir John Wheeler-Bennett has said, inconvenience and dilapidation were the keynotes. The finest room in the house, the lofty and noble saloon designed by Sir Jeffry Wyatville as a dining-room for George IV, had been partitioned into three with scant regard for the ceiling height or the line of the panelling. The Duchess went from room to room, exclaiming how simple it would be to restore this splendid apartment to its original proportions, sadly truncated and divided as it was. When considered as one room, five superb Gothic windows, with casement doors, would face south-west across the lawns. Additional rooms had been ineptly added, north and east, by different architects to meet the hurried needs of varied occupants. Cupboards built in with brass rails disclosed that three or four depressing rooms downstairs had been bedrooms. There were two accompanying bathrooms, complete with the bulbous fitments and mahogany casing that passed for Edwardian luxury. A second storey had been added above the Wyatville saloon, and the staircase mounted to four other bedrooms and a bathroom.

To the north lay a warren of servants' rooms and a separate cottage, plastered, timbered and tiled in the Norman Shaw style, which served as a guest wing, as one of the guides explained, with two spacious rooms and a bathroom. "We must see everything," the Duchess no doubt suggested, as was her way. And everything must have included a mysterious door and an enticing though perilous flight of stone steps that led downward to the great underground kitchen directly beneath Wyatville's dining-room. It was cool yet unmusty, a wonderful prospective wine cellar. Its vaulted ceiling invited admiration and the explorers exclaimed as generations had done at the enormous old table, six paces and thus six yards long, two yards wide, ten inches thick, which had occupied the middle of the floor for a hundred years. Having been originally lowered through the floor of the apartment above, no one could get it out again, and so there it stood in scrubbed prim perfection.

The party then retraced their steps and we can picture them, inspecting, discussing, planning, in the sun room that ran off the conservatory, and in the adjoining octagonal room, a parlour of painted timber and glass, that formed the south-west corner of the house. They perhaps passed through one of the splendid casement windows of the saloon onto the terrace, shaded beneath a glass-roofed, rose-wreathed verandah. They visualised the lawns expanded and widened, cleaned of the more fulsome and aggressive shrubs. In the south garden the rose pergola flourished in high summer luxuriance and, near at hand, they found Mrs. Fetherstonhaugh's aviary cages, empty now, but full of future promise of pet birds for the children.

The visitors saw that the Royal Lodge would do, whatever the difficulties to be overcome. "It is too kind of you to have offered us Royal Lodge," the Duke, on returning to London, wrote at once to the King. "Now having seen it I think it will suit us both admirably."

They had resumed their summer holiday at Glamis when the King replied from Balmoral. "I am so glad to hear that both you and Elizabeth liked *the* Royal Lodge and would like to live there," he wrote, underlining his words decisively. "I hope you will always call it *the* Royal Lodge by which name it has been known ever since George IV built it."

III

In any other walk of life Queen Elizabeth the Queen Mother — the then Duchess of York — would have been called a born home-maker. "Elizabeth could make a home anywhere," her husband once remarked with pride to their old friend, Lady Airlie. An ability to set a transforming, improving hand upon her environment, enhancing its tranquillity and charm, was in her blood. Her mother had come as a bride to the decaying Hertfordshire mansion of St. Paul's Walden Bury, its elegance and form hidden by a mantle of ivy, and had fully restored its eighteenth-century graces. Her father, the fourteenth Earl of Strathmore, when faced with the disposal of an unwanted family property in Durham, first re-examined the house with a keen eye to its attractions and earmarked some of the more notable architectural features to heighten the feudal atmosphere of his Scottish home.

A vast seventeenth-century fireplace, replete with shields, coats of arms and heraldic figures, was airily transferred to Glamis Castle, and there set in an apartment graced in turn by an impressive ceiling of simulated Tudor plasterwork. In their London home in St. James's Square also, the Strathmores made the most of every moulding and pilaster in a mansion by Robert Adam. Never were Adam fireplaces better matched

15

with accessories, graceful alcoves better filled with flowers, or windows draped with more regard to the sheen and colours of the painted ceilings: painted, as it happened, by Angelica Kauffman. Within this atmosphere of refinement and good taste, the youngest daughter of the house was bed to the assurance that she, too, would one day preside over a gracious, smoothly run and happy home. The difficulty was that, in falling in love with a royal prince, Lady Elizabeth Bowes-Lyon also fell a victim to all the housing difficulties to which princes are heir.

The British people cherish a romantic wish that their princes and princesses should marry happily, but characteristically fail to make any provision for their married life by arranging to house them with modern ease. Public money can be lavishly spent in creating a cranny for a King and Queen in any one of six or seven palaces, but as soon as the need of accommodation arises for the next generation of royalty, expenditure is narrowly watched, estimates pared, questions raised in Parliament, and the officials responsible for public works and buildings impose their own deterrents of counter-proposals and delay.

In 1923 the Duchess of York had walked down the aisle of Westminster Abbey as a bride still with some remaining uncertainty as to where she would live after her honeymoon. Queen Mary favoured White Lodge in Richmond Park, her own childhood home; Frogmore House in Windsor Home Park was proposed, and the newly-weds spent a day or two of their honeymoon there as if to try it out. The Home Park is the smaller precinct below the Castle, and Queen Mary had happy memories of living there in summer in earlier days, enjoying "the occasional crowing and cackling from the poultry yard." But neither the hens nor the proximity to the royal tombs near the lake appealed to the new Duchess of York. It may have been dismaying to find that she was expected to live so publicly close to her in-laws, steeping herself in the same feudal atmosphere.

Although the King had one hundred and forty-five grace-and-favour residences at his disposal, all but two were either occupied or considered unsuitable. The swollen total seems large, but included the fifty-seven homes provided for the widows or next-of-kin of war heroes at Hampton Court, the eight service cottages attached to Marlborough House, the eight convenient apartments for royal kinsfolk and courtiers at Kensington Palace and the sixteen suites at Kensington Palace where other members of the Royal Household or royal relatives could enjoy the perquisite of living rent free. There are also forty-six "g & f's" at Windsor Castle, divided among the staff, the clergy and the so-called lodgings of the Military Knights, the veteran army officers housed, in recognition of distinguished services, in the picturesque Horseshoe Cloisters. But for a newly married princess, as the Duchess of York became in status, the housing shortage was clearly acute.

The grace-and-favour residences were regulated with particularly adroit diplomacy by Queen Victoria's private secretary, Sir Henry Ponsonby, back in 1881, when the Government took over the repair and maintenance of all the surplus messuages — including Royal Lodge — in return for a very large reduction in the Civil List. The Queen continued in complete control of the surplus space, and could alone nominate the tenants. But the Government was henceforth responsible for structural and external maintenance, and also internal maintenance and repair — putting into good decorative order, so to speak — on every change of occupant. The grace-and-favour tenant pays no rent and their residential responsibility is limited to rates, tenants' repairs, fire insurance and the cost of lighting, heating and water. In some cases, a tenant may even secure an allowance towards these bills in return for services within the royal establishment.

Queen Victoria stipulated at one time that her grace-and-favour tenants should not winter abroad, but this ruling long since became a dead letter. It is hardly surprising if these desirable residences are rarely vacated in the course of a lifetime. When the problem of the Duke and Duchess of York's accommodation still remained to be solved, nieces and grandnieces of Queen Victoria had already held the tenancy of the ground-floor garden suite at St. James's Palace for sixty years. Clarence House, seldom decorated externally, stood half-empty and unheated, visited only once or twice a year by Queen Victoria's son, the Duke of Connaught, then in his eighties. His sister, the aged Princess Louise, occupied the largest suite in Kensington Palace. For the young and charming Duchess of York there was indeed no alternative to White Lodge, Richmond, which at least enjoyed an open view across the Deer Park. But the Yorks remained in residence at Richmond for barely a year before they became convinced it would never suit them.

The decorations were supervised by Queen Mary, in fact, while the young couple were still on their honeymoon. The Queen took charge without remembering what a thorn in her side *her* mother-in-law had proved in arranging the bridal furnishings at York Cottage, Sandringham, nearly forty years earlier. When the new Duchess of York returned to London and White Lodge in June 1923, it was to discover that little more remained to be settled than the placing of her wedding gifts and personal belongings.

Within three weeks, the bride had to face an ordeal of inspection when the King and Queen came to lunch and Queen Mary toured the whole house to see how she had arranged everything, but the verdict was favourable. In King George's eyes, his new daughter-in-law could do nothing wrong, as he strolled with her down the curving Green Corridor or stood behind the ironwork balcony of the Blue Room to admire the view. "They have made the house so nice with their presents" he wrote afterwards. Similarly visiting the newly-weds, the Prince of Wales, who had been born in the house, mischievously opened the doors of sundry small closets and claimed with high spirits that the house was "commodious."

The domestic amenities of every kind had, however, scarcely improved since Princess Amelia, daughter of George II, first lived there; and the cumbersome and inefficient pipes of the central heating installation had changed little since the regime of Queen Mary's plump and well-upholstered mama, the Duchess of Teck. A tradition lingered that Lord Nelson, paying a visit from Merton, had sketched the battle-plan of Trafalgar on a small study table "with a finger dipped in wine," and the family joke was that he used wine because the ink was frozen. The Office of Works undertook to provide a new boiler but the chilly draughts of October swept the house and the promised improvement still failed to arrive. The Duke and Duchess were driven to rent The Old House at Guilsborough in Northamptonshire for the winter, ostensibly for the hunting but perhaps equally for the heating as well.

The spring was already bringing milder weather, indeed, and the Yorks were within three weeks of the first wedding anniversary before the Duke could write triumphantly to his mother that the workmen had installed the boiler and "marvel of marvels they worked on Sunday!!" But with all the commitments of a brilliant post-war London social season, White Lodge was proving hopelessly inconvenient as a base. To avoid appearing before vigilant eyes at a State function with her frock crushed by the long car ride into town, the Duchess had to change at her mother's new house in Bruton Street. Happily, another temporary solution was at hand. Her sister-in-law, Princess Mary, was in retirement while awaiting a baby and proposed the loan of Chesterfield House, her Mayfair home, an offer which the Yorks gladly accepted.

Through her sister-in-law, the Duchess also first heard that the Crown Estate mansion of 145 Piccadilly was falling vacant and eagerly "put her name down" as a possible tenant. At Glamis, at St. Paul's Walden Bury, at White Lodge and Chesterfield House and at Sandringham and Balmoral, the Yorks had now become hardened as any inveterate travellers in the art of living out of suitcases. When in the winter of 1924–25 they embarked on a long tour in East Africa, a safari indeed entailed no extra discomfort. Living under canvas, the Duchess would startle her party by appearing at the evening meal chic and fresh as if she had not been "creeping through thorn bush and wading waist-high in a swamp" only fifteen minutes before.

In vexing contrast, it took three years of protracted negotiations and deferred repairs before 145 Piccadilly was ready for occupation. At one time, Curzon House was rented; and when the Duke of York heard in the autumn of 1925 the wonderful news that his wife was to have a baby, he hurriedly arranged to take a furnished lease of 40 Grosvenor Square. But as all the world knows, the baby girl — Queen Elizabeth II — was born at 17 Bruton Street, the double-fronted mansion which had become the London home of the Duchess's parents. One may look in vain for the house today, for it was long since demolished. The site is straddled by the massive Berkeley Square House, and we can visualise the birthplace of Elizabeth II only as a point in space, somewhere in the building, above the premises of the First National City Bank.

IV

The young Duke and Duchess of York moved into 145 Piccadilly on their return from a world tour in June 1927, and thus established the clearest landmark of all on the road, lined by temporary homes, which they traced on the way to Royal Lodge. As with 17 Bruton Street, the thin four-storeyed, not unimpressive mansion has completely disappeared. Much of it was decisively erased by a bomb in the Second World War; and east of Apsley House the traffic sweeps into Hyde Park precisely over the spot where it stood.

As with White Lodge, too, the Duchess was again denied the pleasure and fun of day-to-day supervision in transforming the empty house into a home of her own. She studied sketches of colour schemes, it appears, in the battleship *Renown* on the way to New Zealand and was in Australia while the painters were picking out the pattern of her drawing-room ceiling in gold. In the reception rooms the double doors were capably painted flat white with gilt mouldings to Office of Works (Royal Palaces) specifications, the chandeliers hung; and perhaps the patterned carpets alone represented the Duchess's own personal choice. Perhaps it was the Duke's decision to place his ninety-pound elephant tusks on either side of the entrance hall, but it was appropriate that visitors to the Duke of York's official residence should be reminded of his Commonwealth travels.

A morning-room on the ground floor served as waiting-room to the Duke's adjoining study, and the Edmund Brock

21

painting of Princess Elizabeth over the mantelpiece hinted that the house was, after all, a family home. Behind its high windows on the first floor, the drawing-room typified its period with the fringed lamps, mantelshelf bronzes, armchairs slip-covered in brocade, gilt-framed mirrors and lacquered cabinets. The Duchess's little sitting-room next door was altogether simpler, "chintzy … massed with family photographs" as one visitor recalled. A member of the household tried to recollect the "nice, homelike, unpretentious" atmosphere years later, and could define it only in sound: the muted hum of the London traffic giving a sense of inner calm and tranquillity, the canaries singing near the garden door, a clock that chimed with a sweet carillon and, later on, the sound of children's voices drifting bell-like and magnified, down the staircase from the nursery floor.

As soon as the little Princess Elizabeth's great liking for horses became apparent, toy horses on wheels began to gather on the topmost nursery landing, beneath the glass dome, until there accumulated a stable of thirty or more. Among the visitors to these realms were two Uncle Davids — one the Duke's elder brother, then styled the Prince of Wales and later still as the Duke of Windsor, and the other the Duchess's younger brother David Bowes-Lyon. When in doubt, each donated a horse.

Playing space around the house was no problem. At the back, beyond a small courtyard constantly swept by cooking fragrances from the kitchen ventilators, a small iron gate led out to the shrubby enclosure of Hamilton Gardens, a private playground for the line of Piccadilly mansions wedged between Hyde Park and Park Lane. The little Princess toddled here sometimes, clasping her nursemaid's hand, and for alternative diversion there were the gardens of Buckingham Palace, which could be reached only by car, or the spacious beatitude of weekends at St. Paul's Walden Bury, her grandparents' home in Hertfordshire.

Although the Duke and Duchess of York lived at 145 Piccadilly for nearly ten happy years they had not made it their home for three years before the Duchess again experienced the roseate visions of the house-hunter and inevitably began to dream of a house with a garden filled with birdsong and windows open to the summer air. In 1930 two factors gave sudden clarity and direction to the daydream. One was the birth of Princess Margaret, and the Duchess could talk contentedly of the need of a garden for the children. The other factor, as quirkish fate decreed, was the fun that the then Prince of Wales was having in fixing up Fort Belvedere.

"A castellated conglomeration," as the Prince called it, an old Georgian folly on the southern fringe of Windsor Great Park, near Sunningdale, had fallen vacant the previous year, and the heir to the Throne lost no time in asking his father if he could have the grace-and-favour lease. "What could you possibly want that queer old place for?" said the King, in surprise. "Those damn weekends, I suppose? Well, you can have it."

Probably the Prince of Wales and his brother pored over the plans together. One of the bedrooms of the highest tower opened on to the flat roof of a lower tower, providing an unseen hideaway with a superb view, a perfect adjunct for the principal guest room. The provision of three other intended guest rooms, each with its own bathroom, would leave little bedroom space for the Prince himself but he airily disposed of this difficulty. A one-time entrance hall of indescribable shape should become his bed-sitting-room. An adjacent stairway, which formerly led to excessive storage space in the cellars, was now to descend to a Turkish bath, with medium and steam rooms and convenient showers.

If some of these proposals aroused mocking family derision, the Duchess could sympathise with her brother-in-law's plans for built-in cupboards or dressing-rooms to fill every awkward nook and corner. The Prince dealt sympathetically with the past, but in his own room the Gothic French windows were to be changed to a run of modern casements, and ill-fitting shrunken wooden windows elsewhere were to be replaced with draught-proof steel. For the drawing-room, a room endowed with great character by the felicity of being eight-sided, a fashionable interior decorator submitted a scheme for scumbled paintwork to simulate old pine panelling on the plaster walls.

Tumbling out in sparkling enthusiasm, all these ideas stimulated the Duke of York's own innate architectural interests and deepened his wife's resolve to find and make a place of their own. The Prince of Wales was to confess that he felt caged in London, in his official home quarried into St. James's Palace, and he grew weary of living in other people's homes at weekends. The enchantment and airy atmosphere of the Fort provided the gay and volatile mechanism of escape. "The sheer pleasures of creation took possession of me," the Duke of Windsor has written. "I found a new contentment in working about The Fort with my own hands — planting the herbaceous borders, moving shrubs ... building a rock garden with cascades pumped up from a dam... I pressed my weekend guests into arduous physical labour ... but presently they began to share my enthusiasm. Even my brother Bertie would come over to lend a hand."

But these were the days when the Prince of Wales never dreamed that he would become Duke of Windsor, that he would relinquish the throne to his brother Bertie or that Royal Lodge would become the future royal arcana instead of Fort Belvedere. The desolate aftermath of the Abdication was to cast a veil of sadness and disrepute over the Fort until Mr. and Mrs. Gerald Lascelles restored it to laughter and happiness when they took up the Crown lease in 1955. Yet at the dawn of the nineteen-thirties nothing had tarnished the magic, and even Queen Mary came over to see the Fort with the Duke of Gloucester. "At 3 Harry and I went over to Belvedere to see David's garden, we then walked with him thro' the Cedar Walk which he has improved by cutting away laurels etc to the Ruins — David came back with us to tea…"

Probably Queen Mary did not meet Thelma, Lady Furness, at the Fort. Lady Furness has since written unstintedly of her royal romance, the nights in the pre-Simpson era when she felt herself "inexorably swept from the accustomed moorings of caution … each night more completely possessed by our love." But Jane Austen could not have demurred of the scene on many weekends when Thelma and the Prince sat together working on petit point, Thelma copying a Dutch flower painting to make a firescreen for the Prince, her host working upon an embroidered paperweight for his mother with at least seventy-three shades of yarn, the theme a royal crown, while Thelma's father, Harry Morgan, sat reading aloud from Walter Scott.

Family patterns are expressed in virtues and faults alike. The Prince of Wales' persuasive exhilaration in hacking undergrowth and "clearing acres of dark laurel" was to be echoed in Queen Mary's wartime wooding parties then years later, attacking ivy and undergrowth at Badminton, and we can see that it led directly to the rejuvenation and great gardening projects of Royal Lodge. In the early summer of 1951 the

Prince of Wales was engaged in transforming a muddy lily pool below his mock battlements into a swimming pool complete with new flagstone paving for the sunbathing chairs, and walled alcoves for shelter. Stirred by these improvements, the Duke and Duchess of York must have motored the scores of miles of roads in and around Windsor Great Park, scanning Georgian lodges, fishing temples, farms, cottages, all occupied and almost all ill-fitted for their needs. Thus it was with a sense of marvelling opportunity that the Duchess heard that Mrs. Fetherstonhaugh had decided to leave Royal Lodge.

Like the Fort, the Lodge had its own aura of private enclosure and seclusion. Like the Fort, the Lodge boasted a dining-hall designed by Wyatville for George IV. By more preposterous chance — for the two establishments were founded sixty years apart — the homes of the two brothers each had octagonal living-rooms where one could stand gazing out upon two magnificent old cedars. The droll amusement of coincidence need take us no farther.

2: THE YORKS

I

The British people have always observed a markedly dualistic attitude towards its monarchy, weighing its royal personages against the dross of gossip as well as against golden loyalty, readily acclaiming them at coronations, jubilees and weddings but criticising sharply with the next swing of the pendulum. King George V quietly celebrated the twenty-first anniversary of his Accession, in May 1931, and in that same month a great bank crash in Vienna brought the heavy breakers of economic depression sweeping across Europe. Three months later the King had to advise his Prime Minister to form an emergency National Government composed of all political parties. The run in the banks, the abandonment of the Gold Standard, and the axe of retrenchment, all followed in sequence. The King surrendered £50,000 from the Civil List and the Prince of Wales contributed a similar sum to the Exchequer, but scandal and questionings were not unheard.

It was not an auspicious moment for a royal couple to begin home-making. The announcement that the Duke and Duchess of York were to take up residence in Royal Lodge was made in *The Times* on November 21st, but first the newspaper indicated that to make a financial saving the Duke had sold his six hunting horses, obtaining nine hundred and sixty-five guineas by auction at the Leicester Repository. As the Duke wrote to the Master of the Pytchley, "It has come as a great shock to me that my hunting should have been one of the things I must do without." To a friend he wrote more privately of the "damned hard facts" that had to be faced. In acquiring a house, the

27

Duke was somewhat in the position of a young man being sternly reproved by his bank manager.

The mere cost of bullets, as well as beaters and entertainment sufficed to discontinue shooting in Windsor Park that winter. "I can't afford it," King George V wrote, and it required optimism on the part of the Duchess to dream her dreams of Royal Lodge. All she needed at first was simple modernisation and redecoration, with the conservatory demolished to make space for two extra ground-floor rooms, with bedrooms above, but whether any part of the expense might be borne by the Office of Works remained doubtful. At Fort Belvedere, under the far less stringent national finances of a year or two earlier, the Prince of Wales' accountants had succeeded in assigning only part of the cost of plumbing, redecoration and the provision of new steel casements where the south-west windows were most affected by the gales. The Prince was privately forced to meet most of the £21,000 expenditure from his own bank account, and the Duke and Duchess realised they could not hope to fare better at Royal Lodge.

By March, 1932, however, the financial tension was already easing and *The Times* again felt able to remind its readers of the Yorks' prospects at Royal Lodge, "They will take possession gradually... They will stay a night or two towards the end of May and later will spend much of the summer there." In reality this announcement no more than reflected the young Duchess's optimism that bricks and mortar could be conjured into place as fast as thought. Less innocent souls could smile on reading in June that the Duke and Duchess were "not moving in until the early autumn because the alterations to the house have proved to be more extensive than was anticipated." In the interval a London firm of builders and consultants had arrived on the scene and confronted the Duke and Duchess with the firm realities of good building practice.

The firm was William Willett, whose staff and consultant architects, Frank Webber, F.R.I.B.A., and his assistant, Frank Day, A.R.I.B.A., knew perfectly how to distil a client's most impractical wishes into tangible drawings and sound specifications. On reviewing the service accommodation, and on discovering that certain walls were no more than a brick thick, the Duchess had to revise her idea that she wanted only a new wing on the site of the conservatory. New staff quarters were essential, and with each expansion of the plan, the Yorks must have feared that delays threatened to extend interminably into the future. At one stage, the young couple thought it would be pleasant to move in quietly during the autumn of 1932 before work was finished. But we soon find this amended to "probably November, 1932, after returning from Glamis." Once, during the feverish but unavailing house-hunting that followed a particularly trying month at White Lodge, the Duchess supposedly sighed that it would be pleasant to live anywhere, "even in the Queen's Dolls' House." Curiously enough, this is nearly what happened. The fates, though hard of hearing, are often obliging; and the Duchess found that her daughter's playhouse was ready for occupation long before the adults could move into Royal Lodge.

II

The odyssey of the Little House, Y Bwthyn Bach, is an amusing story in itself. It was nurtured by the idea of Queen Mary's Dolls' House, that fabulous miniature, one-twelfth normal size, sometimes reported to have been a national offering by the British peoples to Queen Mary, but originating in reality as a more personal tribute by a number of friends.

The gift had gained celebrity throughout the nineteen-twenties, and in 1930 a group of Cardiff businessmen similarly decided that it would be a good idea to express affection for Princess Elizabeth with a house made to miniature child size as a gift from the people of Wales.

One need not omit the ingredient of Welsh pride. Craftsmenship, artists and designers of the entire United Kingdom had contributed their talents to the faithful microscopic perfection of the Queen's Dolls' House. The Little House was to be a reproduction of a traditional Welsh thatched cottage, adapted to a scale of two-fifths ordinary size and exclusively of Welsh workmanship.

Shortly before Princess Elizabeth's fifth birthday, the Lord Mayor of Cardiff, an Alderman Snook, wrote to the Duchess of York to enquire whether such a gift would be acceptable. The Duchess not only expressed delight but tactfully suggested that it would be a pity for the enjoyment of such a house to be reserved for her daughter alone. Would it not be a charming idea to first put the house on display for some good cause?

This precisely fulfilled every Welsh hope. The house would be a wonderful draw for the Ideal Home and Building Exhibition to be held in Cardiff later that year. The Cardiff architect, Mr. Morgan Willmott, A.R.I.B.A., submitted plans for a double-fronted house, twenty-two feet wide and eight feet deep, sufficiently miniature and yet imposing as the main attraction of an exhibition hall. It was not a doll's house, the publicists were at pains to stress, but a royal home "wherein the little owner could spend many happy hours practising the domestic arts."

To the left of the entrance hall was a dwarf living-room about seven feet square and, across the hall, its opposite room was a kitchen of about the same size. The rooms were four feet six inches in height and at the press preview conscientious journalists were seen for the first and only time going round a royal home on their knees. There were four rooms, and it occasioned no surprise that Y Bwthyn Bach proved to be an idealised version of a prosperous Welsh suburban home of the nineteen-thirties adapted as a royal toy.

Only the plumbers found it unorthodox that, instead of a bathroom over the kitchen, the owner's bedroom was above the kitchen and the bathroom inconveniently placed over the living-room on the other side of the stairs. The forty-inch bath was probably never intended for any use except the ablutions of washable dolls but to allow for plenty of splashing on the part of the junior mistress of the house the hand-basin, a normal twenty-two inches wide, departed sharply from scale. It is said that the Princess alone ultimately noticed that the chimney above the thatched roof was a dummy, linked with neither flue nor fireplace, and she would airily explain, "One doesn't need fires in summer."

The first youthful viewers at Cardiff accepted the fantasy at face value. Admission was reserved for children under ten, some of whom were difficult to winkle out of the house, and attendant hostesses were forced to sit on stools in the rooms like giantesses to help keep the crowds moving.

The spectators found the nineteen-inch-high table in the living-room set for dinner with sparkling glass, porcelain and napery, the Welsh dresser decked with buttercup-yellow china, the miniature longcase clock truthfully chiming the hours. In the kitchen, the twenty-inch gas cooker, wash boiler and stainless steel sink were of correct child height. The cabinet-makers had been proudly photographed beside their bedroom furniture before installation, the oak wardrobe note reaching their shoulders, the top of the chest-of-drawers level with their knees. The bed, four feet long, complete with sheets and pillows, blankets and coverlets, was of practical intention and invited a child's afternoon nap; and the bathroom was complete to the embroidered "E" on the bathroom towels.

Delighting in the project, the Duchess of York sat to Margaret Lindsay Williams for her portrait to be hung over the living-room mantelpiece and went shopping with an eye for smaller treasures. A case of one hundred and seventy-two pieces of hand-made miniature cutlery formed a sideshow at the British Industries Fair that year. The spoons and forks were of solid silver, the knives of stainless steel, and the Duchess could not resist buying it when she subsequently saw it on display at Harrods.

Firmly constructed of timber beneath the rough-cast, the Little House went on tour to Bristol and Birmingham, and raised thousands of pounds for charity before returning to Wales. The conservatory at Royal Lodge had been demolished by then, but rebuilding had otherwise barely begun when the Duchess went to Cardiff in mid-March to receive the title deeds of Y Bwthyn Bach and crouch her way round the rooms on a tour of inspection. In a mood of high comedy, the Lord Mayor handed over a miniature insurance policy, explaining that the cottage and contents were covered against fire and flood for £1,250 and that the annual premium of £6 11s. 3d. had been paid as a gift by the insurance company. With mock gravity, the Duchess expressed her hope that the risks would never arise; and no one dreamed that within a week the Little House would be in flames.

Swathed in tarpaulin, and loaded on to a ten-ton trailer behind a steam tractor, the house left Cardiff by road at midday that Sunday and spent the night, not inappropriately, on Chepstow racecourse. Contentedly throwing out sparks and smoke, the steam engine chuffed north next morning until near the River Wye, seven miles from Monmouth, the driver saw the glow of fire in his driving-mirror. The timbers of the Little House had been fireproofed but not the tarpaulin. The blaze instantly spread to the thatch and flared like a haystack.

While the driver rushed frantically to a telephone, his mate and a passing A.A. scout did what they could with extinguishers. It is on record that "the Monmouth Fire Brigade arrived within four minutes of the phone call and laid a hose to the river" and the affair was treated like a national disaster. The Lord Mayor of Cardiff "summoned his committee of control to an emergency meeting" and *The Times* next day solemnly announced that "letters and telegrams of sympathy reached the Lord Mayor from all classes of people."

The insurance company, too, nobly sent a cheque that same day in full settlement of the £750 value of the structure. (The furniture and effects, having travelled by separate lorry, were undamaged.) The insurers had, in fact, settled over-hastily, and the cheque was happily returned "as making good would cost nothing like that sum." Never were there such courtly business manners of such promptitude, for the architect ordered materials for repairs on the afternoon of the fire and the builder re-engaged his thatchers and ordered two tons of straw for the roof. Unchivalrously, the immediate hurry was not Princess Elizabeth's approaching sixth birthday but the impending London Ideal Home Exhibition at which Y Bwthyn Bach was to make its debut, a mere two weeks off. It was fortunate that the fire-proofing had proved highly effective. The British public learned within the deadline that the three thatchers and other craftsmen worked day and night to keep the reconstruction in progress; and thousands of people peeked through the windows of the Little House at Olympia to find it pristine and good as new.

Next, as if defying fate, the Little House was delivered to the Royal Lodge site on May 11th and set on its prepared foundations on Friday, May 13th, without mishap. It took fifteen years to ripen the coincidence that the house originally chosen as Princess Elizabeth's first married home, Sunninghill Park, was also damaged by fire before she could occupy it.

First introduced to her house at the end of May, the little Princess was entranced with it. So were her parents, hunched at their first command tea party in the white-panelled living-room. Welsh pottery ornamented the mantelshelf and the small format of the Beatrix Potter books, including one in Welsh, proved just right for the bookcase. A midget radio set filled the house with music, and even a wireless licence had been thoughtfully provided in the dresser drawer. The kitchen cupboards held not only brooms and brushes of proportionate size but also saucepans and cookery gadgets, mixing bowls, baking powder and flour.

Everyone, indeed, found the Little House delightful. It was the first thing that the Princess took her new governess to see when Miss Marion Crawford joined the household the following year. Throughout "Crawfie's" tutelage the two children looked after the house themselves, cleaning, dusting, polishing, and learning by doing, "more than any domestic-science school could have taught them" as Miss Crawford said. Whenever a visit came to an end, they solicitously put away the blankets and linen, wrapped up the silver to preserve it from tarnishing and hauling dustsheets from a little store box to cover the furniture. Peeping into the house by invitation three or four years later Lisa Sheridan noticed the shining brass and silver, everything spotless, everything in its proper place. The hall table, she noted, held a tray for visiting-cards and a little bowl of fresh flowers and "everything in this elegantly furnished house reduced, as if by magic, to enchanting proportions…"

III

The Little House was set in the small garden, secluded within yew hedges and rose pergolas, originally created by the Fetherstonhaughs or their predecessors, just to the south-east of Royal Lodge. Curtained from the entrance court by cypresses, junipers and mature rhododendrons, this sequestered corner formed the favourite retreat of the Yorks when they came to inspect the work on the main building, which progressed — as the economic crisis abated — by ever faster leaps and bounds. Pruning, planting, weeding, they began the taskwork of gardening, at first partly initiation and partly a refresher course, that was to provide an unfailing source of mutual happiness and recuperation for the next twenty years.

It became their habit to motor down from town on every Saturday morning that could be spared. A picnic basket would be placed in the boot of the car, the children needed no second bidding to climb eagerly into the back seat with Alah or Bobo (Miss Clara Knight and Miss MacDonald, their nannies) and off they would go, a family party.

The morning would usually see discussion with the various consultants at the Lodge with the Crown surveyor, the men from Willett's, the architects or interior decorators and others, who found the Duchess of York a client who knew her own mind. Whatever the architects — the "two Franks", Mr. Webber or Mr. Day — may have thought or even hinted, for instance, they had to respect her firm instructions to leave the

35

old glass-roofed verandah just as it was, but for repair and repainting. On a less conventional note, the Duchess wished to have her bedroom and dressing room on the ground floor, close to the entrance lobby. It would obviously be pleasant to be able to stroll on one level, straight into the early morning freshness of the garden; although, for security, apparently, a proposal of a direct garden door was declined. Still more to the point, the Duchess foresaw how convenient it would be to be able to arrive from London and go straight to her bedroom mirror before meeting guests.

Week by week the Duke and Duchess greeted the progress they saw with increasing enthusiasm and praise, and the carpenters and painters worked overtime that summer. Occasionally, in bad weather, the royals would bivouac in the great saloon and lunch amid the smell of fresh paint. More usually, with the week's problems settled, they would retire, away from the sawing and hammering, to the surprises of the picnic basket in their own pleasuance.

The Fetherstonhaugh grounds had embraced sixteen acres but now ninety acres were included within a tall chestnut fence. The afternoon was often devoted to planning new walks and rides through the woods. The Duchess remembered the pleasures of her childhood at St. Paul's Walden Bury where the lawns ended in green avenues that ran into the woodlands and now, in quest of that elusive dream, she and her husband tackled the briar thickets and bracken to open the first new tracks up the gentle slope of the hill. As a new beginning, also, to train the eye of her own children, she planted a sprig of twisted willow, *Salix matsudana* 'Tortuosa', and as she said, "It grew like lightning," its twisted twigs and branches so like a Chinese painting. Queen Mary, too, on one of her visits, mentioned a house-warming gift for the house, something old for something new.

The gift when it arrived turned out to be a shaped and weathered piece of stone, a pedestal, indeed, from the demolition of old Waterloo Bridge. The little Duchess caught the note of sentiment and thoughtfully placed the memento by the path that divided the settled garden sanctuary of the Little House and the point where the shrub-besieged lawns of the Lodge awaited their own changes of destiny. Later, embellished by a fairy figure, it became a notable feature of the children's gardens.

3: THE TRANSFORMATION

I

The Duke and Duchess of York quietly moved into Royal Lodge in the autumn of 1932, probably in November, while workmen were still pottering in the guest rooms, and shortly after they returned from Glamis. Henceforth the Lodge was to be the young couple's real home, as Sir John Wheeler-Bennett has said in his official biography of King George VI, "the home they could make for themselves, of which the keynote was to be gaiety and love and laughter; above all, a home where their children might grow up with boon and blessing of a family life replete with affection and understanding, such as the Duchess had enjoyed and the Duke had never known."

The western block of George IV's saloon or dining-room stood as it had done for just over a hundred years, with the exterior of the sun-room and octagon room to the south washed a decisive white, walls and woodwork alike, and outwardly little changed. Beside it, the new eastern wing on the conservatory site suggested rose-coloured spectacles, the stucco painted a soft rose-pink, the woodwork lavender-grey. There had, in fact, been differences of opinion on the shade of the colour-wash. The Duchess decided to give both a trial, but the white was of short duration and rose won the day, unifying the saloon with the new wing and reducing the apparent size of the addition. As a romantic touch, the Duchess had picked out the smaller mouldings in gold and had insisted that all the mouldings or string courses, and the crenellations and finials of the roof-line should match Wyatville's work. Only these last adornments, in reality, looked finicky and uncomfortable and were eventually cleared away.

The Duke and Duchess had striven to hint at the past without slavish copying, and both contributed equally to the finished effect. The Duke had acquired a drawing board, with set-square, dividers and other instruments to clarify his wife's ideas and compile his own with exactness and, modestly commencing in architectural practice, it is said that he busied himself with measuring tapes and provided exact requirements on the garages and stables that were to open on to the service drive to the north. From the main gardens the Lodge looked little changed, and this care in detail may suggest why the Yorks had waited so long to move in.

Now they warmed the house with expectant hospitality and the rush of entertainment filled the festive weeks before Christmas. Not many guests as yet could be invited to stay, although eight to ten often sat down to dinner. All the Duchess's married brothers and her sisters-in-law, all the Duke's unmarried brothers were among those early visitors. They may have viewed the Gothic trend of the porch with misgiving — was it to be another stereotyped Office of Works residence? — but once inside the small comfortable hall, the house was welcoming. Two dappled rocking-horses stood side by side in the hall in token of youthfulness, and blossom spraying from a huge vase on the floor seemed to blend house and garden.

It may be true that the Duchess would immediately whisk her closest women friends into her bedroom to the left, only a pace or two away, and mischievously say, "I told you it is a very small house!" For some reason one is always being asked to describe royal bedrooms, as if they were an inner shrine, shielding the ultimate mystery of monarchy. The crimson corridor carpet was exchanged at the doorway, it was reported, for carpeting of misty blue, the furnishing was of simple line, of white applewood, and the coverlet of the large double bed was of blue silk with lemon pleatings. The kidney-shaped dressing table, glass topped, with a square swing mirror, followed the prevalent fashion, and it was a novelty in those days that when one opened the cupboards they lit up inside. One need hardly add that every minor accessory reflected the owner's personality, including the feminity of the Danish porcelain princess flouncing on her pile of china mattresses to one side of the dressing table. It was an amusing representation of Hans Andersen's fairy tale of the Princess and the Pea, and the lower four mattresses concealed a trinket box.

The Duke's room, in contrast, reminded one of a cabin on a ship, with "a blue-green draped bed, very hard looking," as Marion Crawford described it, "a solid dressing-table that itself had a nautical air, and one bookcase..." Not that one need suppose that visits to Royal Lodge commonly began with the bedrooms. Keeping these on the left, the broad corridor runs straight from the painted front door, past a staircase of low broad steps with simple banisters of unstained oak. Then it suddenly turns to the right and here, at the very heart of the house, light floods down from a circular laylight, enhancing the colour of carpeting and flower pictures. The problem of the one dark corner is thus skilfully overcome but, in any case, the range of the octagon room, the former sun-room and the former saloon — now the drawing-room — lie to the left, and one or two doors are always invitingly open.

The octagon room was, as we have seen, a former sun-parlour at the head of the old conservatory. One can hardly recollect this in the friendly, comfortable, luxurious and strangely spacious eight-sided room of today. This was the nucleus of the more intimate family hospitality, and one finds it difficult to recall the original decor, changing as things wear out, though the same in essential character. The prime innovation was the big brick fireplace, to the left of the door, with its wrought-iron log basket and fireback. (The fires were one of the Duchess's first disappointments, for they were inclined to smoke, until the fault was corrected by new patent cowls.)

The three armchairs and three settees seem always to have borne the same soft pink covers, patterned with white flowers, making the room particularly cosy after sunset when the heavy brocade curtains are drawn across the two broad French windows. And was it always the same grey pile carpet, deep and thick for the Duchess's first enthusiastic visitors, but later trodden down by dogs and children though constantly cleaned? Fine gilded leather bindings glimmer on the bookshelves and it is a friendly, secure and comfortable room in which the Queen Mother later spent much of her time, even when alone, working at what was once her husband's desk.

Between the octagon room and the saloon, the old sunroom also shed every skin of its former self, and became known as the Landscape Room. The little Duchess was apt to open the door with a flourish on first showing her guests around. This small rather oblong apartment, used as an occasional sitting-room and, very rarely, a waiting-room, is papered to its full height with scenes of field and forest in fine delicate colourings that pale ivory-brocaded furnishings reduce the walls to an illusion of shimmering space and the pattern continues across the two doors — one to the hall, one to the saloon — so that the *trompe d'oeil* is complete.

The youthful chatelaine perhaps originally intended this apartment as a permanent dining-room. A larger room cheerfully sociable with pale yellow walls and an oval table, was however added north of the erstwhile saloon closer to the kitchens. We need not wander into the modern compact and efficient service quarters. The Duchess had not forgotten the time that it had taken servants to walk along the curving corridors of White Lodge, and at Royal Lodge the provision of a small staff sitting-room on the right of the main corridor ensured a prompt response to the touch of a bell. A convenient planned service staircase similarly led to the upper floors. There were soon to be six main guest suites, excluding the children's rooms above Wyatville's dining-room or the saloon as it came to be called.

We have left till last this *pièce de résistance*, planned by George IV as forty feet long, and perhaps half as wide, and now magnificently restored to these dimensions. Here was early nineteenth-century Gothic not yet divested of its charming Regency inspiration, the panelling painted pale green with major details picked out in milky cream and lesser ornamentation traced in delicate silver. The Duchess was fortunate in the enormous Persian carpet, delicately patterned in intricate blue, gold and rose, that covered nearly the entire floor; and in three superb chandeliers of Waterford glass, each with twelve candles and crystals uncountable, that enhance the lofty ceiling.

Above the green panelling and below the ceiling a gay assembly of small heraldic shields and crests encircle the room like a frieze. At one end the nearly unbroken expanse of wall might have been built for the sumptuous tapestry that hangs there with both rich and soft effect. Yet near to it, below the wall sconces, hangs a picture of St. Paul's Walden Bury, for this is a room of homely reminders and comfort rather than a drawing-room of impressive splendour.

As a careless playwright might say in his stage directions, deeply cushioned settees and chairs stand about. Though details change in time, the settees are upholstered in dark blue and gold, and there are armchairs in gold brocade, a wing chair, and a set of occasional chairs suggesting Sheraton chinoiserie, each in its appointed place without overcrowding. Pedestal card-tables, a grand piano, characteristic French clocks, paintings, and everywhere flowers, contribute to the urbane and feminine atmosphere. On the white stone mantelshelf the Duchess arranged two bronze figures supporting candelabra. A wedding gift, they can be seen in James Gunn's *Conversation Piece* and they are still there today. Another small and graceful clock also stands between them, holding court. It is a clock that might have been chosen to match the taste of the former owner of Royal Lodge whose portrait, framed in gold, hangs above it in the place of honour; none other, naturally, than George IV seen in his prime as painted by Lawrence.

II

When Marion Crawford joined the household the following year, she was always indelibly to remember the simple, home-like atmosphere of Royal Lodge in those days: the birdsong, the perfume of flowers, especially roses, the peaceful daily life. The early morning laughter of the children, the two little Princesses, romping downstairs in their parents' bedrooms; the intermittent tinkle of a tiny bell at the bird table, log fires, cheerful housemaids, these chief elements sprang to the governess's mind, like a Pavlov response, nearly twenty years later.

There were the peaceful lessons in the first-floor schoolroom, at eye level with the cedar branches that dappled the verandah with shade. There were the tranquil hours when

43

Princess Elizabeth went off for her riding lesson with Owen, the groom, back and forth in the circular railed enclosure across the paddock to the north of the house. Mr. Owen endured his share of hero worship from the little Princess and was for years quoted as a minor family oracle with "Owen says…", and then would follow Owen's maxims or the local lore according to Owen. The Duke heard rather too much of it, and once said, testily, "Don't ask me. Ask Owen. Who am I to make suggestions?"

The family at Royal Lodge was markedly youthful in those days: the Duke and Duchess both in their thirties, Princess Elizabeth not yet ten. Miss Crawford came on the scene when she was only twenty-two, while "Bobo", Miss Margaret MacDonald, the nursemaid, played her part in the move to Royal Lodge when still in her twenties. The senior member of the staff, Ainslie, the butler, was not yet forty and in this youthful establishment only "Alah," Mrs. Knight, in serene charge of the nursery world, seemed to possess the timelessness of middle age. On the "home days" when the Duke and Duchess had no need to go to London "Crawfie" and Elizabeth joined them for lunch around the glass-topped table in the dining-room and, at the end of the meal, it was a great delight, Crawfie recalls, to see Princess Margaret opening the door gently, "pushing her small fat face round it."

A warm little hand would be extended for her daily ration of coffee sugar or barley crystals. The elder sister, too, had her quota, carefully sorting out large and small crystals on the table. Then the children would dart through the French windows into the garden for the afternoon session at the Little House, or games of hide-and-seek and horse fairs or charades in the woods. With only the oaks as audience sometimes all three, the girls and their governess, would take turns to act the part of someone they knew and the others had to guess who it was. Although Crawfie has drawn a discreet screen over these games in her memoirs, perhaps Mama and Papa, Owen and Ainslie, Alah and Bobo, grandparents and uncles, came in for their share of dramatisation. These were early exercises in the mimicry for which Princess Margaret was to be renowned ever after.

Lisa Sheridan's discerning professional eye noticed Princess Margaret's remarkable memory and quicksilver responses when she visited the Lodge to photograph the two Princesses. Posterity must now be grateful that the late Mrs. Sheridan's camera caught or devised every possible pose of childhood: the Princesses at the Little House or on the lawn with corgis and Labradors, at the aviary (where some of the budgerigars echoed Princess Margaret's voice) or working near the birdcages in their own special garden, among mountbretias, heaths and azaleas, with their own little tools. There were feeding-bells, painted invitingly with the word "Tomtit" in large lettering, which the Princesses inspected and replenished with fat from the refrigerator of their cottage. At the Lodge, windows stood open, "net curtains fluttering out in the breeze," Mrs. Sheridan noted. "One of them was caught on a rosebush. I remember thinking how closely, in this drowsy bewitchment, this family lived to nature and how easy was the passage from house to garden and back again." The singing of canaries from inside the house reminded the visitor, perhaps unsuitably, of the Palace of the Czars in St. Petersburg where the sound of singing birds filled the glistening rooms with music all the year round. Others found it more difficult to remember that this was a royal family and that a dutiful round of public functions formed the constant accompaniment of private family life.

It was, of course, at weekends that life at the Lodge waxed to its fullest, with the cheerful arrivals of the Duchess's relatives, Strathmores and Bowes-Lyons and Elphinstones, together with visitors of an older, frailer generation such as the Duke's aunt, Princess Victoria, and family callers motoring over from Fort Belvedere and vice versa. We are given a picture of a wintry weekend when Virginia Water, two miles or so south of the Lodge, was frozen over, and the Duke and Duchess of York joined in a skating party with the Prince of Wales, Prince George and others. With her feet unceremoniously thrust into skating boots, a kitchen-chair was produced for support and the Duchess glided over the ice amid gales of laughter. Then there was an afternoon at the Fort when the Prince of Wales produced a newly-arrived package of unbreakable plastic gramophone records, a minor marvel in the days when records were normally made of highly breakable shellac wax.

"Let's see if they really are unbreakable, David," the Duke insisted, skimming a disc into the air and watching it land unharmed on the flagstones. So began an hilarious game with the royal brothers all hurling discs wildly and even evolving a boomerang technique until all the ladies fled to the house for shelter and the game pursued them into the drawing-room. Then a treasured lamp was knocked over by a direct hit and the host called a halt.

But we may note, as the fates may have done, that it was the Duke who initiated this game and his older brother who brought it to an end. Under the blossoming and maturing of his married life at Royal Lodge, the Duke was discovering himself and was more surely master of himself and his environment than ever before. He never ceased to give his wife the credit for their happiness or to speak of "the strength and comfort which I have always found in my home." Whenever the Duke's youngest brother, Prince George, settled down into earnest conversation in the octagonal room, if the talk turned to married life, the young couple would chide the bachelor, "You should try it." Just into his thirties, Prince George, the Duke of Kent, could see for himself that the advice was well-founded. When he married Princess Marina, in November 1934, the eight-year-old Princess Elizabeth was a train-bearer to the bride. The following weekend, a white and silver wedding favour was pinned up in the bedroom of the Little House, one of the first decorative additions that the young owner ever made to the house, and it was still there several years later.

III

To one of his temperament, King George VI began life under a handicap in having an elder brother. Later, this came to seem a blessing, shielding him from the awful looming responsibilities of the Throne, and as Duke of York he hardly dreamed that the burden of kingship would ever be thrust upon him. He was moreover saddled with the name of "Albert," warming in its family diminutive of "Bertie," but stern on the lips of tutors and others. In infancy, his nurse endowed him with the chronic gastric troubles that pursued him for years by feeding methods that often included giving him his bottle during an afternoon drive in a lurching and badly-sprung victoria. Shy and nervous, too, the little Prince burst into frantic tears at the sight of his grandmother, Queen Victoria. "What have I done now?" the old Queen would ask his embarrassed parents. After one of these visits, the old Queen noted in her journal that David was "a delightful child … nice and friendly" but the sobbing Bertie was not mentioned.

His tutors seem to have fallen under the charm of Prince Edward and often made Prince Albert the scapegoat of any brotherly misadventures, meting out blame and punishment which his stammered explanations could not avert. At eight years old, moreover, he was discovered to be knock-kneed and forced to wear splints during lesson hours and while in bed at night. The ordeal can be gathered from one bedtime when he wept bitterly to the manservant, Finch, begging not to have the splints put on, but the reprieve came to his father's ears and was disallowed.

One cannot but contrast this childhood with the unalloyed golden years of his future wife at St. Paul's Walden Bury and Glamis, the adored pet of a large family in which she was the youngest child but one. When Prince Albert was pitched into the Osborne Royal Naval College at the age of thirteen, he had seldom mixed with boys of his own age. The Duke of Windsor was sent to Osborne two years earlier and has given a searing description of the 6.30 a.m. reveille on blaring bugles and gongs, and then the "pathetic crowd of naked, shivering little boys" herded reluctantly towards the Arctic swimming pool an hour before the January dawn. The two Princes took their schooling, and especially the tortures inflicted on them by the other cadets, in good part. But Bertie had to face difficulties without the presence of his adored brother, for the rigid system did not permit a senior boy to be seen with a first-termer and the two Princes were reduced to meeting in secret on the far side of the playing fields when they wished to talk to each other.

The two also had to keep to themselves their skill in *gros point*, an art acquired from their mama when Queen Mary sat with her embroidery on the quiet family evenings. The adversities of the Duke of York must also be weighed against the happiness of boyhood: the long bicycle rides to explore churches and cathedrals with Mr. Hansell, the tutor, the placid afternoons fishing for roach on the pond at Sandringham. "The boy has determination and grit in him," the report came from Osborne College. He failed his final exams, however, and barely scraped through the training at Dartmouth. Tutorial reports still unfavourably compared Naval Cadet Prince Albert with the "keenness and application" of his elder brother.

Yet there were signs, too, of the wider comprehension and sympathy that was to endear the Duke of York to the staff of Royal Lodge and, in his ultimate days of kingship, to his peoples. A story is told by Sir John Wheeler-Bennett of an Osborne captain who kept a small shoot and one day invited a group of cadets to visit him and look at the young pheasants. One of the boys, city-bred and out of his element, made ignorant comments at which the others laughed; but on the return journey it was the Prince who took the trouble to explain the details of the subject to the town innocent.

On the night war was declared, on August 4th 1914, the midshipman Prince — known for convenience aboard ship as Mr. Johnson — was keeping the middle watch on board the battleship *Collingwood* in the North Sea. His letters home reveal his anxiety to see action and he would have been in the Battle of the Heligoland Bight if a sudden onset of appendicitis had not necessitated his transfer to a hospital ship for an emergency operation. This was the first of the illnesses, a heritage from infancy, that interrupted his naval career and sapped his self-confidence. His letters alternately reflect the despondent solitude and introspection of convalescence and moments of jubilant excitement at sea. He was with the *Collingwood* in the Battle of Jutland and under close shellfire. "I never felt any fear … curious but all sense of danger goes," he wrote exultantly to his brother. But within three months a duodenal ulcer led to another operation. His final transfer from duty at sea was inevitable and he was transferred to the air wing of the Navy. In 1918 he became a training instructor at Cranwell and here one of the medical officers was Louis Greig, whom he had known on the *Collingwood* and at Osborne.

Dr. Greig and his wife had taken a small Lincolnshire cottage four miles from the camp, a happy development as it turned out, for Prince Albert was able to move in with them, and would hurry home from the hutments and hangars of Cranwell to mow the lawn or help dig in the garden. He built a chicken-run, trimmed the hedges and had probably never been so happy before in his life. "I feel a different person," he wrote to his mother. It was his first experiment in shaping his environment, the first enjoyable step on the road to Royal Lodge.

We have made this digression in an attempt to stress the intense self-fulfilment which the Duke of York found in developing his own country home. He was never to become a garden contractor's unwary client or a fair weather gardener, content to leave details to his staff, demanding a blaze of bloom whenever the sun shone. He and his wife found an opportunity for discussion, joint agreement and self-expression in the positioning of every shrub. Although contractors were called in after the Duke and Duchess had coped on their own for four years, it was more to help speed the progress of their dream and combine garden and architectural planning to their precise needs. "Now that really is my garden," he once said, after he had become King. "I made it ... go and see it." Meanwhile, on wet days, the Duke sometimes sat at his drawing board in a little room he used as his office to the right of the main door and sketched the next stage in the remodelling of the Lodge itself. This was to be a guest-wing facing the forecourt which would mask the less sightly domestic ramifications of the saloon. He could make his first-draft sketches like an architect, and, as one of his architects has said, he could read a plan like a builder.

The Duke seems to have paced out the length of the bachelor guest-wing at Sandringham in deciding on the broad sweep of frontage that would face the main drive. In 1933 and 1934 these pipedreams for generous hospitality remained unresolved. But before one's home could be complete even a Prince had to indulge in castles in the air.

IV

While the Duke and Duchess of York were arduously clearing the grounds of Royal Lodge in those first winters, they were also very much aware of something going on just to the south of them. Lorries burdened with reels of rabbit-proof netting would drive into the park as if approaching the Lodge gates and then veer to the left and south. Blue woodsmoke hung in the air, rising from a dense thicket of wild rhododendrons, elders and bracken. If the snap and crack of burning laurels alarmed the Duchess, the park foreman, Harry Wye, was reassuring, "It's in the bog — it's the clearance."

Harry Wye and his men would be seen on their bicycles every morning moving into the theatre of activities, where an area of a few acres was being fenced. The lower ground of Royal Lodge itself benefited from a ditch which had been cut to drain the swampy southern fastness and from the tributary of a stream. At an early stage, of course, the Duke of York met the driving spirit behind these developments and heard his plans in every detail. Mr. Eric Savill had been appointed Deputy Surveyor of the Windsor parks and woods in the same

51

year in which the Duke had taken possession of Royal Lodge, and they were both of about the same age. To further this first bond, both had been at Cambridge together after the war, the Duke at Trinity, Mr. Savill at Magdalene. Both had been invalided from their first wartime service, Savill after being severely wounded on the Somme, and no doubt the Duke felt that if he had not been the King's second son, the other's professional bent for agriculture and estate management might have been his own.

Savill was formerly an acting partner in his father's firm of land agents and chartered surveyors in Lincoln's Inn Fields before he decided to accept the Windsor appointment and so assume virtual responsibility for an estate of about fifteen thousand acres. Moreover, he already had an intimate knowledge of the Great Park, with its groves of ancient oak and beech and wonderful woodland rides, an understanding springing from a longstanding friendship with Owen Morshead, Librarian Emeritus to the Queen. The two first met on their first day at Cambridge when they were assigned to the same lodgings. Morshead was appointed librarian at Windsor Castle shortly after his marriage in 1926, and Savill became a frequent guest at his home, the Garden House, in the precincts of Windsor Castle itself. In retirement, Sir Eric Savill occupied another modern house called The Garden House, not very far from Royal Lodge itself.

Eric Savill's appointment as Deputy Surveyor came, however, as a complete though welcome surprise to his old friend, and now the two, in different ways, were both destined to guide and counsel the Duke of York. The Duke was at first startled to find huge ponticum rhododendrons being rooted out like bramble, but rhododendrons flourished on the Windsor soil, and ponticum seedlings were to become a menace to the Royal Lodge garden. Savill cleared the wild varieties ruthlessly where they interfered with his scheme. While the Duke was opening up paths twisting through the coppices of Royal Lodge, Savill was forming vistas through a garden sanctuary of newly-created ponds within the Great Park towards Virginia Water.

Whenever the Deputy Surveyor was invited to dinner at Royal Lodge, the conversation was as incomprehensibly laced with the names of rhododendron species as with racing lore in other company. The Duchess of York once named roses, lilacs and magnolias as her favourite flowers to the secretary of the Royal Horticultural Society, and all were borne in mind in the planting. The Duke named the rhododendron williamsianum with its dainty bell flowers and heart-shaped leaves and, as early as 1934 he also ordered R. Augustinii, Barbatum, Cynthia, Alice, Kewense and White Pearl for the Royal Lodge gardens.

Indeed, as he said, he began collecting rhododendrons. He became a recognised connoisseur, swapping names and information. "Nobody could stump him!" it has been claimed, in his specialised knowledge. Once, after visiting the Earl and Countess of Stair, he wrote a "thank you" letter enthusiastically couched in the language of rhododendrons: "…you gave me such an Agapetum (delightful) time… I am overjoyed Eclecteum (to be chosen out) and Aberrans (wandering) Cyclium (round) so many Erastum (lovely) and Arizelum (notable) gardens in so short a time, has left me Charitostreptum (gracefully bent) with a Recurvum (bent back) and somewhat Lasiopetalum (woolly footed)…" Altogether, in this letter, he named forty-one species. Lady Stair, attempting to make a spirited reply in kind, could name only twenty-six. "Your Basilicum (Royal) Highness' standard is protistum (first of the first)," she acknowledged.

Eric Savill had noticed, early in his appointment, that although the Great Park embodied the traditions of a nation of garden-lovers, it contained no garden of horticultural interest accessible to the public, and the Duke, from his earliest days at the Lodge, gave him such enthusiastic support to his scheme for what are now the Savill Gardens that he was soon given a free hand. King George V and Queen Mary came to see the first results of two years of Savill's planning and hard work in the spring of 1934. As Mr. Lanning Roper has said, one can imagine the feverish preparations as the garden was tidied, the bare patches clothed with last-minute planting, every plant carefully grown. The visit began inauspiciously, for the Queen, in passing under magnificent oak at the entrance of the gardens, grazed her toque on a low-lying branch. The Queen glanced reproachfully at the tree but made no comment. The visitors said very little indeed until their inspection was complete. Then the Queen turned towards the anxious Mr. Savill with a smile. "It's very nice, Mr. Savill," she said, "but isn't it rather small?"

It was "the green light, the accolade," and so began, in close unison and harmony with Royal Lodge, the splendid achievement of the Savill and Valley Gardens at Windsor which now cover over six hundred acres and rank probably first among the great landscaped gardens of the twentieth century. The beginning was both unobtrusive and economic. The first primulas, for example, were sent from St. James's Park after they had fulfilled their duty as spring bedding. Some of the clumps were subsequently divided and found their way to Royal Lodge. The first kingcups edging the Savill streams were acquired by Harry Wye in exchange for rabbits, and there are similarly plants of every kind that were given — and sometimes traded — by the Queen Mother.

The close proximity of the two royal gardens, too, is highly apposite. The Savill Gardens are open to the public for eight months of the year and visited by over 50,000 people every year who contribute thousands of pounds in gate receipts towards upkeep and new development. The gardens of Royal Lodge are, rightly, completely private and jealously guarded. Yet both were created at the same time by the same sponsors, endowed with the same beauty in the same climate, and equally reflect the triumphs of modern English horticulture. One garden freely public, the other rigorously private, the existence of the two within the same square mile or so reflect the British genius for compromise.

V

The editor of a leading newspaper once said to me, "The Royal Family constantly faces an insoluble dilemma. The essence of the monarchy is its inner mystery, and yet we expect royalty to lead even their private lives in a constant blaze of publicity. What's more, we're right, for the more you know about them — the present generation, at least, the King and Queen and the Princesses — the nicer they become." These words were uttered early in the reign of King George VI, when some still regretted the abdicated king across the water, and they were intended no doubt to apply the maximum stimulus to a young and impressionable writer. But George VI and his Queen were then still largely unknown, producing only images of handsomeness and charm as they flickered across the cinema screens before their peoples. Royal Lodge itself was no more than a phrase, embodying only a cloudy image of some country fastness. But its young occupants gain our sympathy and comprehension, I think, as we watch them, still unshadowed by the Throne, walking down through the woods to see how the ponds were progressing, bartering plants, reclaiming and making their own garden, often out in the garden before breakfast while the spiders' webs still glinted with dew.

Not that all was ideal in their ideal world. There were the inevitable disappointments and crises from which all home-builders suffer.

Despite the head-shaking of architects and surveyors, the Duchess of York had insisted on retaining the early Victorian — perhaps very late Georgian — glass verandah outside the Wyatt saloon. One day, after a heavy gale, a telephone call to 145 Piccadilly announced a disaster. A heavy branch had crashed down from one of the two gigantic old cedars, and the verandah was in ruins. No one had been hurt, but the damage was irretrievable. Hurrying home to Royal Lodge as soon as they could, the Duke and Duchess found that much of the shattered glass had been swept up, although the lawn still twinkled with fragments. The ripped and fallen posts lay side by side. By good fortune the windows of the saloon had not been broken, and as if in consolation for the damage a full clear light now flooded the splendid room.

Now that the verandah had been demolished without any guilty scruples of vandalism, it obviously did not need to be replaced, and there arose only the problem of the five holes in which the roof joists of the verandah had rested. These left a wound about nine inches square in the brickwork above each of the five Gothic windows of the saloon and the Duke immediately had the happy notion of fitting into the holes a crown and cypher of each of the five crowned heads having links with the Lodge. But the choice of the five involved niceties. George IV for certain, but could one include William IV who had first used the saloon but demolished the rest? Should one include George III who had visited a house on the site before Royal Lodge was built? Could one include King George V, then happily still living? Could Edward VII merit inclusion on the strength of an occasional visit for luncheon?

The Duke had the Melville lithograph of the old original Royal Lodge of 1830 hanging in his bedroom, and the tangible possession of the house had awakened his interest in its past and renewed his sense of history. It is one of the sadder attributes of our day that a hundred people can crowd on to a small housing estate without perhaps one individual giving a thought to the men who once farmed the land or strolled the neighbouring lanes and left their imprint in walls and trees and records. Eric Savill and the Yorks, in planning their gardens, envisaged landscapes that did not exist and could be won only by fruitful planning and labour. The Duke and Duchess similarly were pleased with the transformations in the house and eagerly planned the next phase but they were conscious, too, that their home had an historic, though sometimes humble past, and presently their imagination began to take wing through all the extra dimensions in time.

The Duke dipped into the varied histories of Windsor but was left unsatisfied. The majority of the books about Windsor Castle scarcely extended into the Great Park, let alone to the almost forgotten Royal Lodge three miles to the south. It was amusing to find that Windsor Castle was not built at Windsor but within the more northern parish of Clewer, hence a constant muddle between Old and New Windsor. Royal Lodge itself was closer in reality to the old true Windsor than William the Conqueror's fortified hillock. In choosing to build a fortress near his hunting grounds William transferred the name of Windsor, but he and his successors as Kings of England, the Plantagenets down to the Tudors, continued to pay twelve shillings a year ground rent for the Castle site to the Lord of

Clewer and his heirs. The payments were maintained for nearly five hundred years, and why the rent should have ceased under Queen Elizabeth I, or whether it had long since been pocketed as a perquisite by some royal clerk, remains a mystery.

All this was amusing but irrelevant to the Duke's main quest of the story of Royal Lodge itself. The trail to the past bristled with red herrings and false clues, and the perplexity of ever-changing names daunts the amateur. Windsor had more lodges than there were towers to the Castle: Queen's Lodge and Manor Lodge, Great Lodge and Hill Lodge, Cumberland Lodge, Forest Lodge and Friend's Lodge, Upper Lodge, Lower Lodge… But which lodge was Royal Lodge?

The Duke consulted Owen Morshead. The librarian knew of a link between Royal Lodge and Cumberland Lodge, its neighbour up the hill. Early in the eighteenth century Cumberland Lodge was known as the Great Lodge, and Morshead had but to turn up Lysons *Magna Britannia*, written in 1806, to find: "The Lower Lodge, or Dairy as it was sometimes called, was the residence of Thomas Sandby, Esq., the architect…" The curtains of time were parted a little but the stage remained in darkness. The Duke conceived the idea of writing a private account of Royal Lodge and its history, weaving together the research of spare hours, and Owen Morshead began to furnish scraps of information for the research folder whenever any relevant item came to his notice in the Royal Library. A recently published book on Windsor had breathlessly begun with prehistory, Romans and Domesday all on the first page. But when was the estate of Royal Lodge first carved within Windsor Great Park? When did Royal Lodge first make its bow in history?

Who could guess that the clue lay hidden in the Castle accounts of Commonwealth days, where was fisted "a small decayed tenement"?

4: THE BEGINNINGS

I

When Prince Philip flew in his helicopter over Windsor Great Park, he looked down on an oval-shaped green terrain, more than four miles from north to south and two and a half miles wide. Flying directly south from Windsor Castle he could skim the young trees of the Long Walk and follow that two-mile avenue as if across the bowl of a saucer to its notable southern landmark, the gigantic equestrian statue of George III, the Copper Horse. Hovering above this weathered green monument, the Prince would see the pink flank of Royal Lodge in a wooded declivity half to his left and, some two miles ahead, he would catch the gleam of Virginia Water. This marks the present confines of the Queen's domain, a realm where all the roads save one are private, a verdant sanctuary enclosing the ninety-acre estate of Royal Lodge firm and safe as if it were on an island.

Yet the larger enormous waste of Windsor Forest once ran into six English counties. Though restrained by the Thames to the north as Windsor is to this day, it stretched south nearly as far as Southampton Water. "A dreary desert and a gloomy waste, To savage beasts and savage laws a prey", wrote Pope, who churned out Windsor verse with the native zeal of a local resident. The savage beasts included, as well as the wolf and wild boar, the Norman constables who would strike off a man's hand for poaching, so stringently was the royal game preserved.

Henry III was granting a rare favour when he instructed his Keeper of the Forest to allow the young prince, his son, to "capture any of the beasts he chose" although, eighty years later, the red deer were so rampant that it took Edward III's keepers forty days to round them all up. Richard II was gracious and civilised, and contributing perhaps to the labour force engaged on Westminster Hall, when he ordered his Cheshire archers to kidnap stonemasons, carpenters and labourers in the Windsor neighbourhood for the work of building a forest lodge.

The roughness was not all on the royal side. With the daring of train robbers, a local gangster named Richard Siward and "a multitude of armed men" attempted to ambush King Henry III himself on his way from Windsor to Reading in 1234. The attack was repelled and an edict went out warning sheriffs to beware should they travel hereabouts with "pennies" for the Treasury. Edward I, on coming to the Throne, thought it worthwhile to expend forty shillings for the total wages of twenty horsemen and forty foot to flush David of Uffington and his gang out of the woods. What happened to the criminals cannot be traced but as late as 1585, in the days of Good Queen Bess, a number of "stout vagabonds and masterless men" were raked from their forest hide-outs and shipped to the Low Countries as legitimate cannon-fodder in the war against Spain.

The "wild bulls and cows" of the park had by this time long since been rounded up, the eyrie of falcons reserved for royal use, the lakes stocked with scores of fat bream and hundreds of lesser fish fished from the ponds of the Bishop of Winchester and transported alive to Windsor. Sheep grazed in the park, making it simple for three hundred to be slaughtered for Christmas. Henry VIII ordered his cropped acres to be sown with acorns to provide a contingency of timber for the Navy. But the swamps were turgid and choked with the rushes no longer needed by the cartload to carpet the Castle floors. With the dawn of the seventeenth century, £600 had to be spent on "draining and conveying the water which now overspreadeth divers parts of the great park of Windsor and maketh it unfruitful."

With the mud abated, the park offered the people illicit opportunities for sport, enjoyment and plunder. Old histories report that "the squires and better sort made private keys, and entered like the gentlemen of highest quality; the locks were exchanged to disappoint the multitude of keys, and they broke the fences with as little scruple as the tramps." All the park palings were expensively repaired to prevent the filling of the park with "horses and cattle of persons unknown" but keepers could be quietly bribed and there were still intruders.

Some of the fences extended farther than they should and were torn down and burned by angry villagers, jealous of any infringement of their traditional rights of pasturage. King James once turned fiercely on the Major of Windsor and demanded, "Do I do you any hurt? Why then do you vex me by permitting your poor to cut down and carry away my woods?" The King demanded that offenders should be whipped and a showy new whipping post was built in Windsor town beside the bridge, but the magistrates were inclined to nod and few of the park trespassers seem actually to have been subjected to punishment. The surviving records of imprisonment yield only the brothers Richard and Jeffrey Richbell as sentenced for riding in the Forest at night, and since they rode "with staves and greyhounds" they were flagrant offenders who could hardly be condoned. But King James and his courtiers for their part rode far and wide in the chase and paid no regard whatever to farming crops or recompense for their ruin. Insane in his passion for hunting, obscenely swearing and blaspheming if the run went against him, the King would dismount eagerly when the stag was brought down, cutting its throat and ripping its belly open with his own knife, often standing in the entrails, daubing his followers and himself with the blood.

Hunting became so constantly his preoccupation and his prey were so fiercely protected that the Berkshire Grand Jury complained that the multiplying of the deer would soon leave neither food nor room for other beasts. They voiced a resentment that spread like fire in dry bracken until every neighbouring village threw up resistance leaders ready to hunt in defiance of the King. One might say that the first nick of the blade at the neck of King Charles was made by his predecessor's knife at the throat of the deer.

We read of John Green and William Purse of Egham who killed a brace of hinds in Windsor Wood and on the following day a brace of great stags, while threatening "to stab or shoot the keepers if they offered to come near them." The people's movement of extermination was so strong and effective that when King Charles came to the throne he found insufficient sport for his friends and was forced to hunt squirrels.

Under James I the confines of the park and the various lodges were surveyed and delineated, the heron ponds charted and even the rabbit warrens were expertly mapped by John Norden, but there is still no sign of the cottage or croft where Royal Lodge was to stand. Encroachments into Windsor Forest and into the Park took place here and there, one a holly grove of fifty acres which ultimately cost the Crown £21,000 to re-purchase. Forest laws prevailed, and if a cottager filched a patch of waste for his garden, and tended it unquestioned for twelve years, the overseers might sanction his possession.

More rapid still was the spreading custom that if a squatter could build himself a hut of turf and have a fire lighted and a pot boiled in the rudest chimney, the hut became established as a house and was unassailable except by expensive recourse to law. If the pot had not boiled, he could be ejected without ceremony and his hut destroyed. Many a man taking shelter in the Forest to avoid being press-ganged into the Navy might bribe keepers or surveyors. No doubt there were foresters ready to exercise the Norman *droit d'seigneur* to allow a man and a maid to establish a home. The Windsor district is pitted with large and prosperous estates not only founded on sand but also unequivocally on a palliasse of straw or a mattress of heather.

The paradise that became the Queen Mother's garden would then have been well-cropped open scrub offering little concealment to the settler. Yet there stood near one of the south gates of the park an ancient manor-house which Normans and Plantagenets had occupied as a royal residence and which Edward I and his Queen used as a nursery for their children. As Queen Eleanor, the Charing Cross consort, was married at ten and spent most of her mature life having babies, including twins, large nursery premises were essential. We know that there were rooms sufficient to require twenty pounds of candle wax a night, that there were two chapels, one with space for fifteen clergy, and vanished buildings — including venison-houses, brewhouses, cart-houses, butteries — that spread over three acres. The point is that there were also distant lodges of this estate, and in our game of detection we shall need to watch one of them, the Hill Lodge, at the crest of the hill above the slopes where Royal Lodge was to stand.

II

In all its millennium of royal history, Windsor Park was republican for only eighteen years, but more was erased under the Protectorship than in all the riots, rivalry, forest fires or neglect of all the reigns before or since. Windsor was solidly on the Parliamentary side. The servants walked down from the Castle to join the Roundhead army and there was such destruction in the Great Park that the Sheriff of Berkshire was summoned to Parliament to explain why he had not put down the riots. The Parliamentary garrison of the Castle soon found its pay two years in arrears, and the soldiers shot hundreds of deer for food and carted away fences and felled trees for fuel.

When Charles Stuart was executed, and Parliament made a survey of his possessions, only 953 deer, valued at £1 per head, were left at Windsor and these were doomed in turn shortly to vanish. Two thousand oaks were earmarked for the Navy but five thousand other old and decayed trees were scheduled as "good for little save the fire." All the lodges, walks and enclosures were listed and the park parcelled and leased in various lots, mainly to old soldiers in lieu of their pay. Among them was Hill Lodge, described as "a small decayed tenement", and at the division of the park this decrepit building was awarded to Captain John Byfield together with seven hundred acres as a quittance for sums probably owing to him since the days when he helped to rout the royalists at Marston Moor.

Brother of Adoniram Byfield, one of the scribes of the Westminster Assembly who profited by publication rights as a sort of Cromwellian Hansard, John shared his brother's business acumen and was a man of mettle and some substance. The tumbledown tenement immediately disappeared and the new owner spent thousands of pounds in improving the land and building himself a house which, small and convenient as it was, was a pleasant exemplar of the coming age of Wren.

Captain Byfield however was allowed very little time to enjoy the gardens and pretty apartments of this new residence, Byfield House, as he called it, with his young wife, Anne. He died in 1657 after barely eight years' tenure, and with shameless and unwise haste his widow and heiress married a barrister named John Barry.

This astute and shadowy man of the law clearly considered he was on to a good thing, and so he might have been but for the Restoration. In July 1660, the House of Lords authorised the return of all former royal properties to King Charles II. Soon afterwards the King visited Windsor to find the Castle scarred by the years of military billeting, "ragged and ruinous," crowded with lodgers, and moreover thoroughly dark and unwholesome, while on its knoll across the vale of the park Byfield House glistened invitingly with gracious new stonework and pristine fresh paint.

As early as September 1660, Barry had warning that the Crown officials were discussing his holding, and with a lawyer's eye for technicalities he launched a precipitate programme of autumn ploughing. It would appear that he hoped to time his occupation from the date of the Commonwealth survey of 27th February 1649, giving twelve years when he or his wife could be proved to have tended the land undisputed, but Charles was in the full surge of novelty, adulation and power, and officialdom acted swiftly at his bidding. In January, four weeks before Barry could hope to complete his claim, instructions were issued to enclose the garden and orchard of Byfield and prevent the occupier from ploughing up the meadows. Barry defied the order, and came to his senses fourteen months later in prison, while the lands of the Great Park "with all the houses thereto belonging" returned to the

King and were nominally leased to Sir Edward Nicholas, his Secretary of State.

More than a decade was to pass before Charles II regularly held court at Windsor Castle, moving into his own new and magnificent suite of apartments in the Upper Ward, with their luxuriant painted ceilings by Verrio, the opulent frames and carved cornices by Grinling Gibbons, and everywhere rich and exuberant furnishings. But meanwhile Byfield House was reserved by the King "for his own diversions," and the Ranger of Windsor Great Park becomes none other than Baptist May, keeper of the King's Privy Purse, the confidante of his amours and the man whom Pepys reported shunned by the townsfolk of Winchelsea "because they would have no Court pimp to be their burgesse." Moreover, a warrant required Byfield House to be fenced with "an extraordinary pale" with "a controll and toppe." This was to be a love nest of more than ordinary privacy.

Not ten minutes ride through the woods lay Sir George Carteret's house at Cranbourne, where the King and his brother, the Duke of York, and all the company were once seen to be "all made drunk … all maudlin and kissing one another … in such a maudlin pickle as never people were." But the comings and goings at Byfield were masked with discretion and there were no prurient eyes to note the quality of the lingerie blowing on the washing line, "the finest smocks and linen petticoats of my Lady Castlemaine's, laced with rich lace at the bottom, that ever I saw," as Pepys had sharply noted in the Whitehall Privy Garden.

The King's enamourment of the beautiful Barbara Palmer was at its full flow and when he created her husband Earl of Castlemaine, "the honour tied up to the males got of the body of this wife," the whispering world knew the reason. The Earl flew to France rather than endure his shame — Pepys expected him to enter a monastery — but Byfield stays out of the picture. In London, Charles supped with Lady Castlemaine nightly. She was irresistible, this woman, in her early twenties, to her royal lover ten years older, and so it seems reasonable to suppose her snugly installed at Byfield. When the ladies permitted, Charles was considerate in his dealings with women, and when he married, the secret rendezvous of Byfield House at least spared his wife's feelings.

It was a widely-known difficulty that the love affair with Barbara blazed simultaneously with the marriage negotiations for the little dark-eyed Catherine of Braganza. The aged Queen Regent of Portugal attached a dowry of over half a million with her daughter's hand, and Charles could not resist the opportunity. As it happened, the Queen Regent defaulted on the deal but sufficient remained in cash and kind, sugar and spices and sterling. "I must be the worst man living if I do not make her a good husband," Charles wrote, and climbed into the bridal bed of crimson and silver velvet as though he meant it. The King's marital tragedy was that Catherine remained childless, while Barbara presented him with a bastard son that very summer.

The following year Lady Castlemaine was entertained publicly at the St. George's Day feast at Windsor. Perhaps rustic seclusion did not suit her. She enjoyed making her splash, wearing £40,000 worth of jewels — by seventeenth-century values! — at the theatre, staking £1,000 on a throw at the gaming table and winning or losing £15,000 in a night. One imagines that her cool eyes noted the effect in a goldsmith's parlour when she turned to her maid and directed, "Willson, make a note for this and that to the Privy Purse for money." No doubt Byfield House saw its private share of the scenes, recriminations, quarrels and reconciliations that originated with her extravagance and echoed round London. Ultimately, her financial demands grew beyond the King's endurance and by this time, besides, her sexual appetites were wandering elsewhere and there was a pay-off. Charles amiably created her Duchess of Cleveland and endowed her — at little expense to himself — with Queen Elizabeth I's fantastically spired and turreted palace of Nonsuch in Surrey. Historians have indicted her as an unscrupulous vandal, for she lost little time in selling the great structure to a builder, who dismantled it for its rich materials, and then the Duchess sold off the parkland in lots. But with Hampton Court, Windsor Castle, Byfield, and Audley End, near Newmarket, Charles had no need of another rural retreat and he had perhaps foreseen this very denouement.

There is a legend that Nell Gwynn maliciously donned black on hearing of her rival's departure. There were other mistresses, notably Louise de Queroalle, the lovely Breton who became Duchess of Portsmouth. The King strode beside her coach one clear frosty day all the miles from Whitehall Palace to Hampton Court, and was thus quite capable of accompanying her on foot from public Windsor to his private hideaway. Byfield may equally be synonymous with the unidentified banqueting house somewhere in Windsor Great Park where the gay monarch and his courtiers enjoyed their *fêtes champêtres*. At all events, merry King Charles resumed the habit of his ancestors in officially residing at Windsor Castle while, in reality, leading a private life devoted to liberty and the pursuit of happiness far from the shadow of its confining walls.

III

There would be justification if the modern occupants of Royal

Lodge had named one of their avenues "King Charles's Walk." The old "King's Ride" passes near the door, and Charles II undoubtedly came this way, striding across the scene of the present Lodge garden, walking vigorously at his "wonted huge pace," tugging out his watch. "Walk with me and hunt with my brother and you will never get fat," he once told Prince George of Denmark, husband of his niece, Princess Anne. And as we watch him on the Royal Lodge scene, his morning constitutional has gravely begun, five hundred strides down the slope from Byfield House.

If his wraith still haunts these paths, it will be an early-morning haunting. Pepys noted soon after the Restoration how the King's early rising discommoded his Court; and the King kept up the habit all his life, no matter what happened at bedtime. On one occasion, his absence at Windsor seemed to promise a lull in a political crisis but the King was suddenly back in town at six in the morning, almost before the sun had reached his beloved wildfowl in St. James's Park, having set off in the small hours by coach.

An endearing man, this tall, swarthy walker. As he marched across the Great Park, enjoying his "mouthful of fresh air," he took keen note of the square coppices of sapling oaks, elms and ashes planted at his command, or he would observe how the fish were rising in the ponds or whether the birds were crowding to the cherries. He would pull off his hat to salute a milkmaid or a ploughman; dogs frisked at his heels but no one was less a solitary walker: he relished a companion and cheerful talk. Evelyn made record of four conversations when the topics ran over astronomy and smoke abatement, architecture and gardening, the behaviour of bees and his collection of curiosities — and Charles, too, had rare anecdotes of his own.

When he was occupied with fishing or planting, or was perhaps preoccupied at Byfield and not to be seen, his Queen Catherine contented herself with alfresco picnics with her household, eating under a tree. We have a report from one of her ladies that "Lady Bath's dish was a chine of beef, Mrs. Windham's a venison pasty," accompanied by delicate baskets of fruit and twelve dozen bottles of wine, "the Queen wonderfully pleased and merry." In the role of a neglected wife, Catherine did not neglect herself, and she enters our record as perhaps the first Queen to enjoy the Royal Lodge glades.

Not that Charles II shunned Windsor Castle. He understood — no one better till George IV — all the facets of outward show that strengthened the image of the monarchy. We find him demonstrating his faith in bread-and-circuses in 1674, when the storming of Maastricht was represented in the Windsor meadows with Olympian gusto and in Hollywood style. A miniature fort was constructed, large enough to hold five hundred troops as its defenders. An attacking force of seven hundred men under the Duke of Monmouth began its approach on Friday, 4th August, and the immense spectacle continued for fifteen days, with intervals dramatically announced as for "the exchange of prisoners." Both Evelyn and Pepys were among the multitude of spectators who watched "great guns fired on both sides, grenades shot, mines sprung, parties sent out, prisoners taken and all the circumstances of a formal siege, all without disorder or ill accident." No better piece of public relations could have been devised for Charles's eldest natural son, Monmouth, and no greater spectacle had been seen at Windsor since Edward I's great tournament of lords and knights nearly four hundred years earlier. This reminder in itself notched a mark for the enduring substance of the monarchy. King Charles seldom missed a trick.

In 1677 the King's new apartments in Windsor Castle were virtually complete, and two years later Mistress Gwynn was given her own house in Windsor Town, its staircase freshly painted by Verrio with luscious "stories from Ovid." Nell's Burford House is not to be confused with Byfield, still aglow with happy, more youthful memories that filled the King's mind. Significantly, when he began planning his greatest contribution to the Windsor outdoor scene, the Long Walk, "an avenue 240 feet wide in a direct line between our Castle of Windsor and the Great Park there," King Charles aligned the walk not due south but directly towards Byfield House. The sixteen hundred elms that he planted for this avenue were still there in full outward magnificence in our own century, though so rotted and dangerous with their 250 years that in 1945, most grievously, they had to be felled. Charles himself saw them only as a broad double line of tender staked saplings, for in the year of the avenue's completion he died of the combined effects of a stroke and the unmerciful ministrations of his physicians, and now a fresh avenue of young trees marks the course of his early walks from his couch to the Castle, and his homeward rides through the dusk and so to bed.

5: GREAT LODGE AND LOWER LODGE

I

In the summer of the Restoration a girl was born who was to bring the early foundations of Royal Lodge into tangible reality. In 1674, at the age of fourteen, Sarah Jennings watched King Charles's make-believe siege of Maastricht and did not realise that one of the heroes of the exploit, a certain Captain John Churchill, was soon to lay siege to her heart and make her his wife. Thrilled as any child at the Windsor spectacle, she would have watched at the side of Princess Anne, who was her friend, and the fates that day were truly prankish, for Churchill was to add lustre to Queen Anne's reign as the great Duke of Marlborough, and Sarah was to be his Duchess.

Sarah's elder sister was maid of honour in the household of the new Duchess of York, second wife of King Charles's brother, James. The two sisters inevitably became the companions of the Duchess's two stepdaughters, Mary and Anne, and between the plump plethoric Anne and the darting, quicksilver Sarah there sprang up one of the greatest schoolgirl friendships of history, a friendship that lingered into at least six of the twelve years when Queen Anne was on the throne. Sarah was the "dear, dear Mrs. Freeman" for whom Anne delighted in playing at being "dear adored Mrs. Morley," names that the Queen invented to establish the harmony of perfect equality. It has been suggested that their relationship was lesbian, as it may have been in juvenile experiment, but at adult levels Sarah was too deeply in love with her husband for an irresponsible passion, and any appearances otherwise spring only from the audacious and extravagant language of the Duchess of Marlborough's own third-person reminiscences:

> … this favour (towards Sarah) quickly became a passion; and a passion which possessed the heart of the Princess too much to be hid. They were shut up together for many hours daily. Every moment of absence was counted a tedious, lifeless state. To see the Duchess was a constant joy; and to part with her for ever so short a time a constant uneasiness — as the Princess's own frequent expressions were… She used to say she desired to possess her wholly; and could hardly bear that she should ever escape…

There is a tradition that the two friends were riding past Byfield House when Sarah, struck by the beauty of its surroundings, expressed a desire to live there, and Anne replied, "If ever it is in my power to grant this desire, you shall have it." Subsequent correspondence confirms the promise: but when was it given? Anne's words convey the assurance of closeness to the Throne. Was it perhaps in the year following the revolution when her father had fled and her sister, Mary, reigned with William of Orange? In the Coronation year of 1688 Byfield still stood empty, and we can see the forthright Sarah descending from her horse to scout around the grounds, and Anne delighted to see the possibility of a gift to express her love. Yet her hopes were thwarted, at least for the time being. Doubtless to Anne's intense annoyance, her brother-in-law, King William, the very next year bestowed the house instead on his Dutch favourite, William Bentinck, who was to become the first Earl of Portland. Here was another cause of the jealousy and ill humour between the royal sisters, Anne and Mary, though Sarah writes that she laboured to keep the peace between them and she herself presumably never made Byfield a source of dispute.

Bentinck was also made inspector of the gardens of the royal palaces and granted £30,000 for laying them out afresh. Apparently the cash was not intended to cover him at Byfield House, but we hear of Dutch gardens which were laid out there in his time. We also find the geometry of a Dutch garden strangely entering our tale. Inspecting his pleached hedges, Bentinck could not have dreamed that the passage of another 250 years and six generations would find his descendant, Queen Elizabeth the Queen Mother, tending her own garden at Royal Lodge, only the proverbial stone's-throw away.

William Bentinck's tenure was brief. Within twelve years William and Mary were dead but Queen Anne, very much alive, was proclaimed in March 1702, and promptly appointed old Sir Edward Seymour to "the fine lodge at Windsor" within the following month. But that Seymour, comptroller of the Royal Household, was a useful nominee to disguise favouritism becomes apparent in Mrs. Morley's immediate letter to Sarah, her new Keeper of the Privy Purse, Mistress of the Robes and Groom of the Stole. Mentioning the departure of the Earl of Portland from Byfield, she explained, "puts me in mind to ask dear Mrs. Freeman a question which I would have done some time ago; and that is, if you would have the Lodge for your life, because the warrant must be made accordingly; and anything that is of so much satisfaction as this poor place seems to be to you, I would give dear Mrs. Freeman for all her days."

Sarah astutely secured the house not only for herself for life but for three lives, intending the other two to be two of her daughters, whom she sadly outlived. Queen Anne's hands were so securely tied that, when the two ladies of equality at last quarrelled, Sarah remained securely in possession, of Windsor Lodge, as she called it, "the most agreeable to me of all the places that I ever was in." With the Lodge and other perquisites, there also went the Rangership of the Great Park for three lives, which gave Sarah a sense of proprietorial rights when Anne came riding over from Windsor for the delights of tea and talk with dear Mrs. Freeman. The Queen skimmed through the park in a one-seater, one-horsed vehicle, a mere basket between high wheels, which she drove herself at furious speed. Swift reported to Stella that around Marlborough Lodge, as he called it, were "the finest places for nature, and plantations that ever I saw: and the finest riding upon artificial roads made on purpose for the Queen."

While Anne lived in a modest house within the Castle walls, "a footstool to the castle," Walpole dubbed it, "a small hot box" that made her husband, Prince George, gasp for breath, the Lodge was a cooling elixir, "no place more agreeable," as Sarah said, "in the three warm months, tho' the house is not large." This turn of phrase was not mere modesty. An old print gives an impression of a small square two-storey house, only six windows wide on the frontage after Sarah had added two for an extra wing, with the roof pierced with dormer windows for the servants. One sees Sarah leading her admiring friend through the newly-furnished rooms, here explaining why white paint with red damask "looks mighty handsome," here expounding the absence of "fret work in my ceilings," the cornices kept simple, "my taste having always been to have things plain and clean from a piece of wainscot to a lady's face."

Sarah's letters written at Windsor Lodge and elsewhere are full of such details. "I have looked upon the Damask by daylight," she writes, in approving upholstery and matching up materials, and in ordering feather beds she specifies "Swansdown, all good and sweet feathers, even for the servants." It was unwise however, she explained, to sleep upon swansdown while the feathers were fresh and still retaining dampness. Exchanging their homely wisdom, the two ladies would have made an unimpeded progress through the house, for neither had patience with bulky or pretentious furniture. Sarah once got down on her knees to measure a bedroom floor. "… so little a room," she pronounced, "should not have a bed in it either broader or longer than necessary" and mirrors were employed to heighten an illusion of space.

Shortly after Sarah's husband was created Duke of Marlborough in commemoration of the victory of Blenheim, the Turkish tent used by him on the battlefield was set up in the garden of the Lodge, furnished with "a carpet to put upon a table and a great carpet to lay upon the ground" and chairs that the Duchess thought "whimsical, odd things." Embroidered with silk and wool, the tent in its day enjoyed a celebrity akin to Montgomery's caravan so that visitors to a fete waited for hours to inspect it at sixpence a head. But, for the present, Mrs. Morley and Mrs. Freeman sit within their tent and enjoy their cheering glass undisturbed; and perhaps, long before Sarah became crippled by gout, there was a summer afternoon when they strolled down the hill to inspect the new dairy built by Sarah near the woodyard. "I remember that Queen Anne never brought any children likely to live till she took that method of drinking … a great deal of milk," Sarah once advised one of her granddaughters. The dairy was on the present site of Royal Lodge.

II

The Duke of Marlborough, in his twenties, had courted Sarah passionately. They remained in love with each other till the end of their days, and the verbal tradition survives that on coming home from the wars he ardently "pleasured" his wife before taking his boots off. Much of their married life was spent at the Lodge, the Great Lodge as it became known among local folk without intending irony. It affords a superb paradox that the Marlboroughs made the snug prim little Windsor house their favourite home during the prodigious, interminable, preposterous building of Blenheim Palace, that gift from a grateful nation which was to cost half-a-million pounds.

One is tempted to picture them, during one of those fleeting spells of idyllic happiness when Marlborough was home from the Netherlands, sitting down together in their cosy retreat to study the architect Vanbrugh's first designs. The Lodge, at all events, was one of the headquarters from which, at her husband's behest, Sarah harassed architects, landscape gardeners, treasury officials and lawyers. Blenheim was the Duke's potent dream but never Sarah's, who came to regard the whole project as extravagant madness. The phenomenal edifice was to occupy seven acres of floor space and courtyards. Stone quarries in the locality were exhausted; the foundations of new additions were laid while all but finished pavilions still remained unroofed, and even the architect drastically altered his scale, a change necessitating the demolition of yards of wall already built.

When Sarah grew out of patience after four years of difficulties and delays, she took on the building of Marlborough House as her new town house in London as if determined to demonstrate that she could do better. Appointing Sir Christopher Wren as architect, she gave directions that the house was to be "strong, plain and convenient … and not to have the least resemblance of anything called Blenheim, which I have never liked…" But even Wren could not please this exacting client. In the end architect and patron parted company and Sarah finished

Marlborough House herself and shrugged aside the £50,000 cost: "almost incredible," she noted, "but not really so extravagant as it appears, because it is the strongest and best house that ever was built."

It is surprising to discover an association between Marlborough House, home in our own century of Queen Mary, and Royal Lodge, home of her Queen successor, and the link is less fragile than appears. Sarah formally laid the foundation stone of her new London home in June 1709, and the following month saw her position at Windsor reaffirmed by a patent which names among her grants both Hill Lodge and Lower Lodge. In the former we recognise the small decayed tenement of only sixty years earlier which became Byfield House and then Windsor Lodge. This is the first we learn of Lower Lodge as an attachment, and its inclusion may indicate that perhaps Sarah had already built it, without the formality of written permission, as a guest or servant annexe just below her lawn near the dairy.

To heighten the confusion, park keepers talked of it in their casual country way as the "little lodge" to the Great Lodge or as the "lower lodge" to the Upper Lodge on the hill. Historians in turn have muddled it with a Little Lodge in the Windsor Home Park, just below the Castle, later occupied by Sarah's grandson as Duke of Marlborough. We are scarcely concerned with the fog of names, except that Lower Lodge was the clear predecessor of Royal Lodge. The self-same foundations, where they stood, were incorporated by Nash in the groundwork of George IV's Royal Lodge a century later.

Sarah's patent, in any event, was confirmed none too soon. Before Marlborough House could be roofed, there occurred her final irrevocable breach with Queen Anne. Hardly was the mansion completed than the Duke and Duchess were relieved of all their official posts, save only the inalienable three-lives Rangership of Windsor Great Park. Nothing stung Sarah more than newspaper allegations that this was a source of profit. "The whole park can witness that I don't make a shilling from it," she retorted, "or take away the little Advantages of the Keepers, most of whom have many children, and what could be so wretched as to take what I don't want, to make others half-starved?"

Her advantages were, rather, solaces in kind. Sharing her husband's temporary exile in Antwerp, she wrote to a friend, "If you should happen to have a mind to take the air, when you happen to be in the spleen and can't bear company, I beg of you to go and see my Lodge in Windsor Great Park where you will find a very clean place and everything that is convenient, and nobody but a housemaid, the gardener, and the keepers, that will ride to fetch you anything you want at Windsor."

The tide of adverse circumstances turned with the accession of George I. But Blenheim remained unfinished in June 1722, when the Duke of Marlborough, dying at Windsor Lodge, breathed his last in a summer dawn. Presently his body was borne by night, escorted by a detachment of Horse Guards down the hill past the Lower Lodge on the way to Marlborough House where he lay in state. Seven generations later the body of his descendant, Sir Winston Churchill, was carried through London in a funeral procession of equal pomp and honour.

Without her husband, the widowed Sarah found Windsor melancholy and unendurable, and the following year she bought an estate at Wimbledon. But the new estate afforded no relief. She pulled down a half-finished mansion, engaged Lord Burlington to design another, was displeased with this structure and demolished it in turn, only to find that her Lodge in the Great Park still held her heart. "I am come to this place, which is extremely pretty in my opinion," she wrote from Windsor Lodge some years later. "If it was not for the convenience of seeing one's friends so easily at Wimbledon, I should repent me of having built that house." In three years more, repentance had strengthened to revulsion. "Came yesterday from Wimbledon. Though it stands high, it is upon clay, an ill sod, very damp and, I believe, an unhealthy place which I shall seldom live in, and consequently have thrown away a vast sum of money upon it to little purpose."

We find Sarah at Windsor Lodge later on, elderly, gouty, sleeping ill, riding to Sunninghill to drink the chalybeate waters at the well, or sending to the keepers for deer suet with which to soothe her legs. She proposes a scheme for ploughing up two hundred acres of wasteland every year but no reply comes from the Treasury, and she protests vehemently "Nothing is to be got by being Ranger of this Park but the fattening of a few runts (sheep) to eat, and milk from the cows... I have the honour of paying all charges of furnishing a great deal of venison for His Majesty's service..." At one time a storm broke around some relatives permitted to occupy Lower Lodge, a quarrel which writers have at times confused with Little Lodge in the Home Park. Sarah gave her tenants notice and then fell into renewed rage on the departure at finding that they took with them not only their furniture but also shrubs and benches from the garden. Many tongues wagged around the affair and Walpole reported that the Duchess had a puppet-show made with wax figures to represent the offenders, including a puppet lady of fashion shown carrying off a chicken-coop under her arm. It scandalised the world, entertained Sarah's guests and must have satisfactorily vented her spleen.

The years crept round. Her granddaughter, Diana, was advised by physicians to spend more time in the open air, and wrote to ask if she could borrow the old Turkish tent. The old lady ordered her butler, John Griffith, to look it out with its furnishings and must have beheld the ravages of time with sorrow. Rats had gnawed holes in the chairs and, as she wrote to Diana, "There is some brass thing lost which fastened the tent together." Griffith was nevertheless instructed to pack it up for the carter. "The chief value of it is to think that it was your dear Grandfather's tent, when he did such wonderful things to secure the nation from being enslaved by the French king..."

III

At the age of eighty-four, Sarah was still waging her battles of Windsor on all fronts only a month before her death at Marlborough House. She was still plaguing the Treasury with demands that they should reimburse expenses which were after all, she insisted, laid out only on behalf of His Majesty King George II. "If they think anybody will do it honester or cheaper than I have done, I shall be very glad to quit the allowance," she wrote to Mr. Scrope of the Treasury. "I would have quitted the Park long ago if I had not laid out a very great sum in building... The Keepers send me word that it has been so bad a season this year that I must buy a great deal of hay for the Deer or they will be starved this winter. For though 'tis a great park, it is full of roads, and there is nothing beautiful in it but clumps of trees, which, if Mr. Pelham does not prevent it, will be destroyed by the Cheats of Surveyors, which in a great measure I have prevented for more than forty years."

Sarah represented that she had paid all the charges of His Majesty's Park for at least eight years, besides a loss in George I's time when she "paid the keepers out of her own pocket because they were so poor." It was typical of Sarah to use that word "pocket" instead of "purse," but she managed other estates in twelve counties with the same unremitting fierceness, and at last it was all proving too much for her. "Give me directions how I am to proceed," she wrote, "and I hope you will allow me sometimes to be in the vapour against Knaves and Fools, which I hate." At St. Albans, her birthplace, lived an old bailiff who had often said in sentiment that he wished he might die when the Duchess of Marlborough died. It made a good newspaper story in the *Daily Advertiser* when as near as could be calculated he died at the very hour that Sarah, Duchess of Marlborough, suddenly fell dead of a stroke.

She left, as one might expect, a long but uncomplicated will in which everyone who had been attentive to her in old age was remembered. Even the men who had carried her sedan chair in London were to be given £45. Her laundry maid, Kate Garmes, must have rushed breathlessly down to the dairy with the news that she had been left a year's wages. It transpired, too, that Sarah in widowhood had bought an estate a year, handling each new acquisition with an imaginative flair for every potentiality. After purchasing the manor of Noke, Oxfordshire, for instance she had the mansion pulled down and several farmhouses built with the materials. The furniture at Windsor Lodge itself was specially mentioned in her will, and left to her grandson, Jack Spencer, who was also otherwise her chief legatee and succeeded her as the third life in the Rangership.

Jack had in fact become the apple of her eye, although she looked dubiously on his casual ways and once complained petulantly, "he is always dressed like a keeper or a farmer." She admired his outbursts of frank temper, so like her own, and opined that he had good nature, sense and many desirable qualities, but when this was said it had to be admitted that he still needed a great deal "to get through the world in the manner that I wish." Jack's defects, however, were to triumph over his virtues with greater speed than his grandmother would have thought possible, and as the new Ranger he barely had time to take stock of the parkland before the *Gentleman's Magazine* recorded his death in June 1746, "at the age of six or seven and thirty, merely because he would not be abridged of three invaluable blessings of an English subject, brandy, small beer and tobacco."

The next Ranger who took up residence at the Lodge before the end of the summer was of very different calibre. That same year William Augustus Ernest, Duke of Cumberland, had fought and finished a battle in forty minutes, leaving one man in three of the enemy dead — many murdered without quarter — on the field. In the same month when he first stalked through the Lodge, his troops were still combing the Highlands for fugitives, burning the crofts, stamping out humble peat fires, scattering or killing their puny herds of goats, nowhere showing mercy. The new Ranger perpetuated the last battle on Scottish soil and was, of course, the Butcher of Culloden.

George II's third son cannot be whitewashed. His "drastic, injudicious methods," to quote one of his defenders, may have insured against a third Stuart insurrection but tourists to Culloden Moor are told to this day of seventeen Highland officers who were confined in a small room for three days and then shot by Cumberland's direct order. One hopes that the patent to him of Great Lodge was a perquisite of royalty rather than a reward.

Happily, our main business now lies elsewhere, down the hill, where the sweet williams blowing in the dairy garden were in reality a reminder of William of Orange more than the grim, satiric dedication that gained currency after Culloden. Attached to Cumberland's civilian staff was a draughtsman named Thomas Sandby, a pleasant self-taught young artist, whose family home was in Stoney Street, Nottingham, but whose life's path was to take him along smoother and better-named thoroughfares. Thomas and his younger brother, Paul Sandby, kept an artistic academy in Nottingham, it is said, when they were both still in their teens. Under this mantle they attempted to glean fees for drawing lessons from one or two pupils and so made the acquaintance of the daughters of Mr. Plumptre, M.P., who seems promptly to have recognised the peril of the two handsome brothers within his family nest and diplomatically countered it by recommending both the artists for situations in the Drawing Office of the Tower of London.

Thomas was only twenty-one when he arrived in London and he drew pay of some three shillings a day, with a concurrent allowance of £91 a year, nearly to the end of his life. Paul, aged seventeen, was less fortunate in securing a sinecure, but both the young men sat down at about the same time to their ordnance drawing boards and both were concerned with mapping and preparing topographical views of service in the field.

Within a year we hear of Thomas appointed as a draughtsman to the Commander-in-Chief, the Duke of Cumberland, during the latter's first campaign in Flanders. The Duke was wounded in the leg — by Austrians who mistook him for a Frenchman — and Sandby assumed light secretarial duties and may have diverted him with some sketches. Duke and draughtsman were both of the same age, and Thomas may have found other diversions. There are family rumours of an early marriage to a girl named Schutz or Schultz, who was probably a kinswoman to another draughtsman of the name on the Duke's staff, although no positive records are known. Volatile and imaginative, Thomas often found it difficult to bring himself to finish anything, a marriage, a map or a drawing. Characteristically, when on survey work in the Highlands in 1745, he was the first to rush the news from Fort William that Charles Stuart had landed, and by way of recognition and reward for this early warning his place was renewed with the Duke as a "personal draughtsman."

The position implied saving the Duke some architectural expenses, and Sandby coped with the architectural plans and specifications of new works at the Great Lodge — henceforth to be called Cumberland Lodge — and at his own Lower Lodge, attached to the dairy, in which he was housed. Paul Sandby, incomparably the better artist, meanwhile continued in survey employment in Scotland where he sketched every picturesque character that caught his eye. But within two or three years he moved into Lower Lodge with his brother, for Cumberland was returned from the Low Countries, and Thomas urgently needed an extra pair of hands and eyes in all the tasks pressed upon him.

IV

"I put a few acorns in my brother's garden at Windsor," Paul Sandby was to write, "and found great pleasure in viewing the opening buds." Paul enjoyed everything, and he assuredly revelled in the scene at Windsor where returned soldiers by the hundred were excavating and planting and landscaping to realise a new royal dream. The rigid squares and circles of woodland that the Duchess of Marlborough had guarded so jealously were felled to allow scope for the new natural plantations that followed the contours of the hillsides. A small stream, the Windles, had long swamped its way through the morass and heath in the southern wilderness of Windsor Great Park, and now equally seemed to afford imaginative opportunities. At some time it had been less aptly rechristened the Virginia, though whether this came from the Virgin Queen, from the paradise that Penn founded or from a house of the name is still a matter of argument. The certainty is that Thomas Sandby noted where springs and rivulets could be blocked or diverted and where a natural basin could be enlarged and dammed and so was formed the handsome lake of Virginia Water.

Under the aegis of the Duke of Cumberland and the Sandbys, it was to be beautified by cascades and grottoes, bridges and belvederes, set against a backdrop of dark, sable firs. Past their door lumbered the ox-wagons dragging out the timber and returning with stone and tiles for Cumberland Lodge. Across the way, a woodyard was a constant hive of activity, and up the hill went the farmcarts, squeaking and jolting, now laden with "thousands of strawberry plants" from Holland, now with "three barrils of seeds" of forest trees brought from America by H.M.S. *Rye*. The Duke of Cumberland's friend, Henry Fox, recorded planting sixty-six different varieties of trees and shrubs at his own home in a season, and the Duke was not behind the new fashion. The race-meetings were renewed at Ascot, the Cumberland stabling magnificently extended to house two hundred horses, including fine Hungarian breeds and splendid Arabians, and the domestic life of the Sandby brothers was set against the constant passing clatter of hooves.

The Duke soon established a menagerie and the cockerels' reveille would be answered by the "very large and curious fowl from Barbary" and even by the roar of lions and tigers. The night could be disturbed by the howling of a wolf, a beast sent as a gift to the Duke with an explanatory letter, "she is as tame as any dog." One wonders whether the Sandbys were disturbed by the African wildlife pecking their hedges, for two ostriches grazed free with the deer and cattle, and the couple can be seen, browsing companionably among the hinds, in one of Thomas Sandby's watercolours of Cumberland Lodge.

The two brothers sketched and painted eternally. They sketched in the courtyards of Windsor and in the scullery of one of its humblest lodges at Sandpit Gate; they took their drawing boards with their travelling pack when visiting friends in London; they tried their hand at horses and dogs, carts and carriages, at empty landscapes in the Great Park and crowded racing scenes at Ascot Heath. They would snatch up an old receipt and sketch on the back, perhaps to please and amuse some passing caller. They drew from life and nature; and one has only to glance over a few of, say, the Sandby drawings at Windsor for the whole of their past scene to come to life with a reality more compelling than any effect achieved by the dubious ghosts of Versailles. Here is bulky one-eyed Cumberland in his long jackboots, his blue coat turned back with facings of red, and his buff waistcoat with military buttons; here are his footmen and servants in their livery of crimson and green; here is Bob Dun, one of the gardeners, weather-beaten, aproned, scratching reflectively with one hand thrust inside his shirt. We see Voules, the bailiff, with his double chins and watchful eyes, clearly laying down the law, and the Duke's agile servant, his livery enhanced with a gold-laced turban. They come before us in their buckled shoes, knee-breeches, stockings, three-cornered hats, or sometimes in rags, as with the bibulous, big-stomached country bumpkin, with poacher's pockets sewn into his blue coat whom we know only as "A Windsor Character." Strolling, talking, conferring, standing in groups in the Great Lodge stableyard, watching a colt put through its paces, we see that the Sandbys have gifted them with immortality, and only their conversation defies our knowledge.

Yet there are flashes, murmurs, whispers, still lurking in unread memoirs. We hear of the old woman who asserted that she had seen "a horse with a white leg running away at a monstrous rate and another horse a great way behind trying to race after him" ... and she was sure that "no horse would ever catch the white-legged one if he ran to the world's end." And what she had seen was one of the secret trials of Eclipse, the prodigious unbeaten horse whose blood is now said to flow in every racehorse in the world.

It is strangely appropriate, when one considers the racing enthusiasms of our own Queen Elizabeth II, so engrossed in horses as a girl, that this king among horses should belong so closely to her own home domain. The tradition is that Eclipse grazed as a foal on the verdant lawn between Royal Lodge and Cumberland Lodge, and an inscription was set up in a paddock nearby, "The celebrated Race Horse ECLIPSE, by Marske out of Spiletta was foaled in this Paddock 1764. He was bred by H.R.H. William Duke of Cumberland." It seems a pity that nothing more can be claimed. Cumberland was one of the original members of the Jockey Club, a devotee of breeding thoroughbred bloodstock, and so phrenetic a racegoer that he rose from his deathbed to attend a race-meeting at Newmarket.

His judgement was at fault however with Eclipse for he sold the colt when four months old for only forty-five pounds, an error all the stranger in that, on the Newmarket occasion mentioned, he saw a win by a filly of the same dam, the first descendant of Marske to run. The great-grandsire of Marske in turn was the famous Darley Arabian; while Spiletta, the sire of Eclipse, was descended from the great Godolphin Arabian.

Illness may have clouded Cumberland's judgement. As a colt, Eclipse was sold to a Smithfield salesman and then entrusted to an Epsom rough-rider who worked him unmercifully and used him for poaching at night, and he was five years old before being raced. Then he won all the twenty-six races and matches in which he took part and at stud altogether sired 344 winners. As for his descendants it has been calculated that a hundred Derby winners in 145 years could trace direct origin in the male line to Eclipse.

One cannot find that the Sandbys sketched him as a foal, although they drew his dam. One could not tell what might catch their eyes: mares in a paddock, spaniels curled up and asleep, the huge turf rollers idly awaiting repair in the wheelwright's shop, and even wagons in the Cumberland yard.

Nor was their scene solely the man's world. Women and children, too, move through their pictures, courtly ladies in dresses with panniers, young women like Mrs. Eyre in her frills and flounces, her fingers poised at a spinet. One charmer in her pink striped dress is seen seated lost in a daydream which we feel we share. And there are young girls walking, girls watched in the wind, watched from behind. The same recognisable characters of Lower Lodge appear elsewhere in different drawings. The pensive girl in pink reappears, for example, on the north terrace of Windsor Castle watching a dog in encounter with a raven. Some of the young people may be Thomas Sandby's own family, for in 1753 he fell in love with the dark eyes of a Miss Elizabeth Venables, who had the distinction of being born in the Piazza of Covent Garden and, buoyed by her comfortable dowry of £2,000, they married and had ten children. (Charmed as one is by discovering the links with the past in one's own family, I cannot refrain from mentioning that the godparents of Elizabeth Jane, their first-born, included William Windham of Norfolk and Lady Jane Cathcart.) None of the ten were born at Lower Lodge, for Elizabeth Jane's arrival coincided with a period of rebuilding when the family were ensconced at Cranbourne and shortly afterwards Thomas Sandby inaugurated a London home in Marlborough Street, where his eldest son, William Keppel, was born. Paul Sandby married in 1757 and had three children, who became happy playmates of their Lower Lodge cousins. In 1786, indeed, Thomas Sandby's fourth daughter, Harriott, married Paul Sandby's younger son, Thomas Paul, and eight of their thirteen children were born in Lower Lodge itself.

One of Paul's drawings which was purchased only recently by the Queen shows us the garden of Lower Lodge, perhaps in 1766, when Elizabeth Jane was rising eight and her brother seven, when there were two younger girls and a boy baby, and there they are, with maid-servants, a pony and frisking dogs under the trees, while a woman, perhaps Mrs. Sandby herself, peeps from the high-sashed garden window of the house in the background. The picture is inscribed "The Deputy Ranger's House." Thomas was appointed Deputy Ranger only the previous year and Paul made several drawings of the house at about this time, as if to compliment his brother's new official status. Beyond the lawn, beneath the immensely tall trees, ash and pine, the house stands pink and luminous, graced with a delicate white-painted entrance porch. Garden-rollers and benches stand about near the flower beds, and against the octagonal bay of the house groups of potted plants soften the brickwork with their flowers and foliage. We glimpse a halcyon moment of high summer, its participants unaware of the coming storm.

Thomas Sandby had meanwhile long since finished his massive improvements of the Virginia River. Workmen were occasionally laid off when the Duke of Cumberland's private funds ran low and he was unable to borrow. His housekeeper sister, Princess Amelia, saw fit to object one day that they did not need so many workmen. "No," replied her brother, "but they need me." No doubt the Duke was equally content to subsidise Paul Sandby in 1754 when his protégé published a series of engravings of the new wonders, the grotto and cascade, the lake, and the mock Fort or Belvedere on Shrubs' Hill that, nearly two centuries later, was to witness the abdication drama of King Edward VIII.

With the addition of a Chinese summer-house, "not exactly a pagoda," to beautify an island, and a humped single-span lattice bridge, designed by Henry Flitcroft of Stourhead fame, this corner of Windsor Great Park assumed at this time the atmosphere of a sylvan world fair. The bridge first evoked wonder as being of a single span of 165 feet, reputed to be the longest single span wooden bridge in the world and "five feet longer than the boasted Rialto." Nearer our own era, the oddity emerges that a nearby inlet was long known as Botany Bay, and blind chance strengthened the coincidence when the Sydney Harbour Bridge was built near that other Botany Bay in 1932 with the world's then longest single-span of 1,650 feet … the Flitcroft measurements precisely multiplied by ten.

As a finishing touch to the Cumberland "delices de Windsore," an old river hulk was transported overland from the Thames, drawn by some forty horses and oxen, to be brilliantly painted, pinnacled and bedizened with banners and bells as a Chinese barge and launched on the Virginia waters as the *Mandarin*. That bright-eyed loquacious old lady, Mrs. Delaney, was rowed out to it with a sightseeing party in June 1757, to admire the quaint craft "as rich and gay as carving, gilding and japanning could make it" and the party walked across the high bridge, "desperately steep … though carriages of all sorts go over it every day." The bridge was so contrived, Mrs. Delaney noted, that "any piece that is decayed may be taken out and repaired without injuring the rest," but perhaps this precaution was neglected. On the night of 1st September 1768, the worst rainstorm within living memory deluged London and Windsor for eight hours, and in the early morning the Sandby household was aroused to the news that the bridge had fallen, the dam at Virginia Water had collapsed and the treasured lake had totally drained away.

Mrs. Delaney wrote eagerly of "the extraordinary inundation. The Virginia Water broke head and is entirely gone, fish and all, and a house in its way carried off as clean as if no house had ever been built there." The old gossip enjoyed the excitement but it was reported that a cottager had lost his life in the disaster, and Mrs. Sandby had the ordeal of watching her husband's frantic anxiety. There cannot have been a day of such shock and terror since the time when a tiger escaped from the Cumberland Lodge menagerie and roamed at large in the park, killing an eight-year-old child.

V

Wits inevitably dubbed Thomas Sandby "Tommy Sandbanks," and a doggerel script circulated the inns, alleging that he had constructed the vanished pond-head of sand and rubbish, lined with clay, like his own cranium, "…what's a head but a noddle? So I think I had best take my own as a model."

One thinks it as well that William Augustus, Duke of Cumberland, did not live to see the calamity. He had been borne to the vaults of Windsor three years earlier and his grand-nephew, George III's brother, the Duke Henry Frederick, was installed as Ranger at Cumberland Lodge. Somewhat of a scapegrace himself, this young man happily made light of the catastrophe. It was a year of torrential rains and resultant disasters. When the Exeter mailcoach overturned at Egham that December, all its occupants and the horses were drowned, and no responsibility attached to Tommy Sandby for that. Local estimates avidly put the damage of the Virginia Water inundation at above £9,000, including £3,000 for making good within the Great Park itself. But Henry Frederick was convinced that his Deputy Ranger could make a fresh start on much smaller estimates and build the largest and finest man-made lake in the kingdom.

Thomas punctiliously expressed his sense of indebtedness by inviting Henry Frederick to sponsor the latest Sandby infant, a girl who was thereupon christened Maria Frederica, the Maria being a tribute to her godmother, Maria, Countess of Waldegrave. In an age of patronage and unrestrained parenthood, invitations to sponsorship offered a promise which Thomas invariably seized for his children. Not all godparents proved as unresponsive as the lawyer, Theodosius Forrest, who sponsored Maria Theodosia Sandby at a ceremony in St. James's Palace and subsequently cut his own throat. Thomas Sandby's eldest son, William Keppel, was sponsored at the font by Keppel, Earl of Albemarle, when aide-de-camp to "Culloden" Cumberland. Such a godfather turned out to be a material advantage when the boy applied for an Army commission, and we later find Major William Sandby of the 12th Foot engaged in the 1782 siege of Gibraltar. Another son, Jeffery Thomas, was guarded from the flesh and the devil by the vows of none other than Sir Jeffery Amherst, commander-in-chief of the expedition for the conquest of Canada, and the improviser of the storming of the Heights of Abraham with General Wolfe. But not every brilliant godparent could ordain a happy destiny. It was Jeffery Sandby's fate to become a lieutenant in the Navy, when he was taken prisoner and wounded in a gun explosion and, shattered and armless, he died in Lower Lodge when only twenty-seven.

It is happier to glance aside at little Maria Sandby's godmother, the fair and buxom Maria, Countess of Waldegrave, "allowed the handsomest woman in England." At his daughter's christening early in 1770, Thomas Sandby probably knew the secret which was stringently kept from King George III, namely, that the formerly widowed Lady Waldegrave was wife to the King's second brother, the Duke of Gloucester. And the lovely Maria, Duchess of Gloucester, makes an acceptable and good-looking wraith in joining the pleasant ghosts in the gardens of Royal Lodge. We can find her likeness in no fewer than seven portraits painted by Sir Joshua Reynolds, whose favourite sitter she was, and indeed a lock of golden brown hair, marked as hers, was brought to light in recent times in a recess of the artist's pocketbook.

Although Sandby could have made her acquaintance as a friend of Reynolds', they probably met through young Cumberland, soon after she became his clandestine sister-in-law by marrying Gloucester in 1766, and there were other links. The three little girls with whom Maria was left in widowhood after the death of her elderly first husband in 1763 were of the same age group as Sandby's daughters, and also in reality of close social equality. Maria's mother, in fact, first steps into recorded history seated on a dustcart before the Bishop of Oxford's street-door in Pall Mall. The Bishop's daughter, we read in a letter from Lady Mary Wortley Montagu, "had the curiosity to call her in merely to see her nearer, and assured me that in all her rags and dirt she never saw a more lovely creature."

Maria, then, was one of three natural daughters born to this waif and Edward Walpole, brother of Horace. When first residing with their father in Windsor we are told that they were ignored by the genteel, until one of the canons of St. George's chapel, Frederick Keppel, son of Lord Albemarle, married the eldest. When Maria, the following year, married Earl Waldegrave, "as old again as she … but for credit the first match in England," the Rev. Keppel himself tied the knot and polite society capitulated. In widowhood four years later she was so beautiful that Eton schoolboys "crowded at Castle prayers" merely to see her, and it is not surprising that she captivated the King's younger brother, despite the otherwise daunting fact that she was eight years his senior and the mother of three.

At all events, the young prince of twenty-three and his wife of thirty-one, with her children, all settled happily together into Cranbourne Lodge; and by some deft sleight of hand with his brother, Cumberland, the Duke of Gloucester became Warden of Windsor Forest. Unlike Gloucester, the young Duke of Cumberland was susceptible to far too many pretty women and at first faithful to none. At Lower Lodge the family must have gossiped of his liaison with the actress Anne Elliot, to whom he "was for two years devoted." They may even have heard whispers of an amorous scandal, perhaps involving a mock marriage, with Olivia Wilmot. But our concern is with the lasting lady of young Cumberland's life, Mrs. Ann Horton, a well-connected young widow whom he evidently met at the dances on the lawn of Sunninghill Wells, "extremely pretty, not handsome, very well made," we are told, "with the most amorous eyes in the world, and eye-lashes a yard long; coquette beyond measure, artful as Cleopatra, and completely mistress of all her passions and projects."

Some ladies looked askance at this Mrs. Horton, with her reputation for leading riotous parties at Vauxhall and Ranelagh, her talk so pointed that, as Lady Ann Fordyce remarked, "after hearing her one ought to go home and wash one's ears." Thomas Sandby, however, joined in the pursuit of her acquaintance with the very best of intentions. The Duke Henry Frederick of Cumberland was married to the amorous-eyed charmer in November 1771, and six months later Thomas invited the Duke and his new Duchess to be godparents, with Lady Amherst, to his tenth — and last — child, Ann Sophia.

Having already carefully named another daughter Charlotte Augusta after George III's eldest daughter, we can be reasonably sure that Thomas Sandby did not know of the King's indignation at the Cumberland marriage, which was to have sharp repercussions at Royal Lodge in the twentieth century. Shocked and outraged, the King called his brother a fool and a blockhead and declared that the woman "could be nothing and never should be anything." (She was, in any case, the legitimate daughter of a peer.) It may be that the King inwardly stormed with jealousy because he had surrendered his own light of love, Lady Sarah Lennox, to make room for his marriage of State with the unprepossessing Princess Charlotte of Mecklenburg-Strelitz, whom he made his Queen. But from this quarrel arose the Royal Marriages Act, pressed forward with unreasoning haste by the monarch whose instability of mind was to resolve into insanity twenty years later.

Indicted at the time for its harshness and cruelty, the Act henceforth made it impossible for any descendant of George II legally to marry before the age of twenty-five without the Sovereign's consent and without the approval of Parliament thereafter. The law did not apply to the issue of princesses who married into foreign families and it was not retrospective. The Duchess of Cumberland therefore was safe and a credit to her husband, for "No woman of her time" as a contemporary noted, "performed the honours of her own drawing-room with more affability, ease and dignity." The lovely Maria, too, was compelled by pregnancy to reveal her six-year-old marriage to the Duke of Gloucester.

There were thus two clandestine marriages, and because of them two godmothers to the two youngest Sandby girls at Lower Lodge. Is it not strange that on the very site of that house, less than two centuries later, the Royal Marriages Act should have been flung with bell, book and candle at our own Princess Margaret in the dilemma of the Townsend affair?

6: THE DEPUTY RANGER'S LODGE

I

The sunlight of life often follows quickly on shadow. Within three months of the catastrophic draining of Virginia Water in 1768, a cherished dream of the Sandbys was fulfilled when George III signed the warrant that founded the Royal Academy of Arts. The brothers were both nominated founder members, with Sir Joshua Reynolds, Benjamin West, William Chambers, Richard Wilson and others and, in addition, Thomas Sandby was elected Professor of Architecture at £30 a year. Paul did even better. Through the Marquis of Granby's patronage he was appointed chief drawing master at Woolwich Military Academy that same year, a post to occupy his time only one day a week at a salary of £150 per annum.

With supplementary allowances, Paul must have felt independent and princely as he sat under the trees in Windsor Great Park and sketched his brother's comely house, with its trim window shutters and neat new fencing, across the way. Thomas, too, confirmed in his appointment as Deputy Ranger under the young Duke of Cumberland, drew Windsor emoluments of £400 a year with an additional £91 half-pay from his surviving appointment at the Tower of London, and found that a will-o'-the-wisp dream that he might become an architect could be followed with more leisure.

Thomas drew designs for "a theatre in Leicester Square" during his earliest days in London, and now the works at Virginia Water were neglected while he competed in designs for such public buildings as the Dublin Royal Exchange. His rival in this was one of Paul's closest friends, an architect named James Gandon, and Paul no doubt felt relieved when Gandon was placed second and Thomas third, with an Irishman — evidently by prearrangement — running off with first prize. In reality, one of Tom Sandby's few architectural clients was the soft-hearted Duchess of Gloucester, for whom he built "a noble edifice commanding a most extensive prospect of the Thames" on St. Leonard's Hill, nearer Windsor. As Grand Master of the Freemasons, Henry Cumberland also obliged with the commission that led to the building of the Freemasons' Hall. But Sandby's dearest project, for a bridge loaded with classical design across the Thames near Somerset House, was never carried out. He mentioned his "bridge of magnificence" in one of his earliest Royal Academy lectures and was heard still dilating on the theme twenty years later. Luckily, no one took him seriously. He built an "elegant" five-arched bridge of stone across the placid Virginia Water which still serves to this day but a three-arched bridge of his across the fast-running Thames at Staines collapsed within three years. Bridges were not his strong suit.

Events went similarly astray when the Duke of Cumberland acquired the ancient stones of the beautiful "Holbein's Gate" from Whitehall, intending to re-erect the structure, probably on Sandby's suggestion, at the end of the perspective of the Long Walk, where the "Copper Horse" stands today. Having sketched the Gate long before in his youth, Sandby had a sentimental interest in its salvation but this task, like so many of his projects, was left unfinished, and the gate ended up as so much building material, its antique medallions built into various lodges in the Great Park. In the midst of so many preoccupations, the repair of Virginia Water was neglected. John Wesley came sightseeing in 1771 and "viewed the improvements" of Fort Belvedere, the "shrubberies and woods having some straight, some serpentine walks." In a little upper study Wesley was pleasurably startled to find many religious books, admirably well chosen. "Perhaps the great man spent many hours there, with only Him that seeth in secret." But Virginia Water remained a reed-covered muddy expanse, commanding no attention.

It was not until the summer of 1789 that soldiers of the 23rd Fusiliers were set to work, bringing gigantic boulders from Bagshot Heath to lend both strength and romantic appearance to the pond-head; and at the Deputy Ranger's Lodge, by then, the Sandby family was facing the stress of changing times. Nearing his seventies, a widower for seven years and an old man, wearing his own white hair, Thomas stares at us obstinately, with a trace of melancholy, in the portrait by his friend, Sir William Beechey. The household revolved around his daughter, Harriott, nineteen years of age when her mother died, who had placidly accepted an injunction Thomas skilfully laid upon her in verse,

> A second parent thus provide
> To Charlotte on this plan;
> Maria may in each confide,
> And all be guides to Ann.

Both the eldest daughter, Elizabeth, and the eldest son, William Keppel, had already married and moved away. Harriott thus becomes the heroine of the family; and but for the boys away at the wars the house must have been excessively crowded when Paul Sandby came down from London, bringing his deaf wife and younger son, Thomas Paul, who was bent upon becoming an artist like his father. We are told by Pyne that, among other duties at Windsor, Paul Sandby, senior, gave lessons in drawing and engraving to Queen Charlotte and the Princesses, and the Royal Library possesses four little sketches possibly produced under his tuition by George IV's younger brothers. Besides filling his sketchbooks with his Windsor drawings, Paul was also induced to model castles until his bookcases at home were stacked with towers and turrets, and probably meals could not always be served without moving some of "Father Paul's" clutter off the dining-room table.

Oddly enough, the Royal Family of that day seem never to have bought or to have been given a Sandby drawing. Six of Thomas's topographical views of Windsor Great Park hung on the walls of Cumberland Lodge until, on the death of the Duke Henry Frederick in 1792, they were consigned to languish in a portfolio in George III's library. Paul lived long enough to hear that many of his brother's works had passed into the royal collection, and many of the Sandby drawings now so treasured at Windsor Castle were bought by George IV as Prince of Wales through the dealer, Colnaghi; but by far the largest royal accession was via the auction at Christie's of Paul's own pictures after his death in 1809. The two brothers slaved for the proverbial carrot of royal patronage to little effect. Thomas teetered on the brink in 1777 when he became one of the two Royal Household architects appointed by the Board of Works and he designed a now-vanished reredos for St. George's Chapel but the appointment lasted only three years. The plum of reconstructing a wing of Windsor Castle for the Queen went to Sir William Chambers. If, as some think, Sandby was responsible for excavation works at the Castle which, according to Walpole, "endangered, aye, cracked the whole range of buildings," it would have been like him.

Yet I think one can accept the testimony of Sandby descendants that King George III, bulbous in eyes, cheeks and stomach, was often in and out of the Deputy Ranger's Lodge, content to sit down without ceremony to a plate of cold mutton and salad. At the court at Windsor all was formality. Poor short-sighted Fanny Burney had to adjust the Queen's buttons and tapes by instinct in her role as Assistant Keeper of the Wardrobe, for it would have been a breach of Court etiquette to wear spectacles. When the Royal Family walked on the Castle terrace, an official was present with a wand "to control individuals from pressing too much" and ladies-in-waiting were expected to remain quite still and not cough, sniff or rustle in the presence of royalty. But at "Mr. Sandby's house" the King could indulge his enjoyment of country affairs and country people, his voice booming "Hey! Hey!" and "Halloa!" at their ever-open door. One of the Sandby daughters used to tell how she and her sisters, on hearing the King in the hall calling for their father, would step out of the low window in the room in which they were sitting and run through the back of the house to change their dresses before making their appearance at luncheon with His Majesty.

Local folk marvelled at the King's faculty, typically royal, for recognising everybody and his knowledge of "the character and affairs" of everyone at Windsor. Paul Sandby enjoyed reporting to his friend, Gandon, the King's remark that "I am never idle, but can turn my hand to anything," an observation probably given force like all the King's remarks by a resounding "What! What!" No doubt the King knew of the soldier husbands of Tom Sandby's daughters. The story spread round Windsor of an occasion when the King, on noticing a woman working alone in a field at harvest time, asked where the other labourers were and was told that they had gone to see the King. "Well, then," said the stout monarch, pressing some money into her hands, "you may tell your companions who are gone to see the

King that the King came to see you, what?" Two of the Sandby sisters, Charlotte and Maria, who survived as old ladies into Victorian times — they lived indeed to see the birth of the future Edward VII — told many such tales to their grandchildren.

II

In his last years, Henry Frederick, Duke of Cumberland, surrendered his title of Ranger to his brother, the Duke of Gloucester, but the post now was as nominal as Thomas Sandby's own deputy role had become, for the King himself took strident command. George III became affectionately known to his subjects as "Farmer George" with genuine cause. Farming formed his escape from the undying animosities within his family, from the feuds and intrigues with his politicians, and from the frustrations of his own conception of kingship.

Sandby had developed the landscape for ornament but scarcely for profit. The renovations of Virginia Water had not improved the old marshy tracts and thickets around Cranbourne Tower to the west. The King began reclaiming 1,200 acres "in the light of reason and judicious experiment" and founded the two great parkland enterprises, Norfolk and Flemish Farms, which remain profitable agricultural areas to this day. When George III wrote letters under a pseudonym to an agricultural magazine, his views were expert. The King took into his service Nathaniel Kent, the protagonist of crop rotation, who had become the chief exponent of progressive husbandry. Kent was a man in his fifties who had found a land valuer's career more profitable than diplomacy, and by publishing a book of *Hints to Gentlemen of Landed Property* had gained an influential and wealthy clientele. No love was lost between the expert, with his advanced talk of Flemish husbandry, and the ailing, bohemian, futile Deputy Ranger. The Sandbys were probably in the habit of keeping a cow on the green pasture of the Lawn opposite Cumberland Lodge. Nathaniel noted with satisfaction in his private journal one day that he had barred the Lawn with a few posts and a chain "to keep off idle people and cattle."

Whether by chance or design, the nucleus of his early measures as royal bailiff was in the stockyards immediately adjoining the Sandbys' garden. Here was raked and stacked the manure to fertilise the newly broken acres which had been ploughed by oxen soon numbering hundreds. Mr. Sandby's yard, indeed, was found so "comfortable for the cattle," as Kent recorded, that his house well was newly piped and pumped to provide water, regardless of the effect on his domestic supplies. The family had scarcely recovered from this annoyance than a new ox shed was built, fortunately on the far side of the yard. Rumour long had it that the Duke of Marlborough had planted trees according to the disposition of his troops at the Battle of Blenheim, but these battle formations now readily fell victim to revenue. In a letter to Gandon, Paul Sandby, senior, expressed his sadness that majestic oaks of Windsor had "bowed their heads to the adze of keen necessity and lust of lucre."

One exception was made in the toll of reputedly decayed oaks which the King ordered to be cut down. This was the venerable Herne's Oak, legendary in Shakespeare's day, where the so-called Herne the Hunter, a park-keeper wounded by a stag, had hanged himself in sudden madness. A line of twelve monarchs and more had spared its gnarled bark, hollowed like a cave and sanctified by tradition. The Sandbys sketched the tree, it is said, while it was still yielding acorns. This hallowed trophy, then, was to have been spared; but the workmen, equally true to tradition, made a mistake and the oak was felled.

Although hundreds of tea-caddies alleged to have been made from "genuine Herne's Oak" appeared in Windsor and neighbouring towns, the King convinced himself that the oak of the legends was really another tree not far away. This deputy tree in turn was blown down in 1863 and Queen Victoria planted another in its stead. Perhaps the local craft of oak tea-caddies will witness a notable revival within another century or two. At another time, Paul wrote with pride that his son also had been a great planter of oaks "having ten living instances of his nurseryship!" These oaks would have been too slender to attract Kent's depredations and evidently survived to help give the substance of continuity to Royal Lodge.

The new pastures prepared on the slopes west of Cumberland Lodge now aroused the interest of Nathaniel Kent and the King in the breeding of Merino sheep. Since so much of the agricultural traffic was routed via Bishops Gate along the old King's Ride, the Sandbys no doubt glanced from their windows to see the first silky flock passing by. Did they realise there were no rams? A homeward-bound British fleet had exchanged compliments with a Spanish fleet encountered at sea, and in the ensuing visits between the flag officers, the Spanish admiral presented to the British admiral some female Merino sheep for sea stock. Being a rarity, the ewes were kept, however, and on their return to England the flock was presented to the King.

But the rams? The Spanish had cornered Merino breeding and the difficulty was that the exportation of rams from Spain was strictly forbidden. The Spanish ambassador in London was approached with the hint that the needful rams might be smuggled out of Spain via southern France and Germany. The envoy refused to play ball, but his wife proved more amenable when offered a pair of cream-coloured Hanoverian ponies of the type which drew the King's gold State Coach, a breed which the King and Queen alone could use. The rams were duly smuggled out of Spain and safely delivered to Windsor, where the dark-eyed Spanish shepherds were briefly seen by the astonished locals gambling with the doubloons and dollars which their enterprise had earned them. Under the auspices of Joseph Banks, the naturalist who had been with Captain Cook on the *Endeavour*, Merino cloth to be "ranked with the best superfine cloth manufactured" eventually crowned the experiment and gratified the King.

When Thomas Sandby died in 1798, Harriott and her husband hoped, despite the drawbacks, that they would be able to stay on in the house that had always been their home, but it was not to be. The Lodge was required for Joseph Frost, the general superintendent of the royal farms under Nathaniel Kent, and the younger Sandbys learned that any protest against eviction would be useless. In some recompense, a grant of £100 a year from the Royal Bounty was made to Harriott and in the emergency perhaps the entire family crowded for a time into Paul Sandby's house overlooking the St. George's burial ground in the Bayswater Road, "a house low and small," as he called it. His eyesight failing, Paul Sandby lived on into his eighty-fourth year. "I endeavour to keep up my spirits," he wrote, "as long as I am enabled to make use of my hands," and a pension from the Royal Academy smoothed his last months of life in 1809. Nathaniel Kent died of apoplexy the following year and so the Sandbys pass from the Windsor view.

7: THE ROYAL COTTAGE

I

In the year 1752, when the Sandbys were putting the finishing touches to the first Virginia Lake, and Culloden Cumberland was rejoicing in his bridges, cascades and other toys, a third son was born to a millwright's family in Lambeth. The boy was John Nash, of Kentish yeoman stock on his father's side, of Welsh blood through his mother. When John was only eight years old, the millwright died and entrusted him to the benevolence of a well-to-do uncle, who could steep the impressionable boy in the amenities of a gentleman's house with its "hothouses, greenhouses, aviaries, canals and basins of water" alongside the river.

Married but childless, Thomas Nash had prospered as a calico-printer, and the six horses mentioned in a will as being in his stable suggest carriages for his wife and himself, besides a riding hack or two and perhaps a pony for his nephew. Riding through the market-gardens that stretched south from the river towards Clapham, young John's interest must have been aroused by the new villas he saw in the course of building. Since Uncle Thomas ultimately left him a legacy ten times larger than that stipulated for anyone else, we may infer John was a favourite nephew. In all probability, his benign uncle detected his interest in architecture and provided the money for him to be an articled pupil in the offices of Robert Taylor, the architect in those days of a part of the Bank of England, and we find Nash in his middle teens serving in Taylor's office, reputedly with Samuel Pepys Cockerell, grandson of the diarist, and other pupils. This gives us his first fragile though inconsequential link with the Prince Regent and Royal Lodge, for when Cockerell in turn took pupils they included William Porden, who ultimately became architect of the Indian Stables of the Pavilion at Brighton.

A story has come down of an office emergency when drawings were needed in a hurry, and Nash drew all night by candlelight and saved the situation. Told by one of his own pupils, it sounds characteristic of Nash's determination and pugnacity, if not his flair for publicity in spreading good stories about himself. As a junior, Nash was able to marry in his early twenties, in enjoyment of regular work as an assistant draughtsman and perhaps supplementary gifts from his Uncle Thomas. It was when Thomas Nash died, and bequeathed him a thousand pounds, rather than a hundred, that the fun began. Nash branched out into speculative building, acquired an old house in Russell Street, Bloomsbury, embellished it with stucco and Corinthian pilasters, but then unluckily failed to find a buyer for this thoroughly remodelled residence in time to satisfy his creditors and he was declared a bankrupt.

Undeterred, John Nash went home to his mother, then living in Carmarthenshire, and whether Nash deserted his first wife or she deserted him remains in question. We know that the penniless and bereft young man went into partnership with a builder named Saxon with whom he secured the contract for providing a new roof and ceiling for Carmarthen Church. To economise on plaster, he thought nothing of grinding down the alabaster of medieval knightly tombs and other antiquities, and this cut-price work won him a commission to design and build Carmarthen Gaol. Pleased with the firm of Nash and Saxon, builders, the vestrymen of Carmarthen were not to know that their ceiling would fall down within eighty years. Meanwhile, Nash received his first professional private fee as an architect by designing a bathroom for a friend. The Welsh country house with a bathroom designed by the original architect of Royal Lodge and of Buckingham Palace has long since vanished but in its place, by a very odd chance indeed, there stands a mansion designed by Sir Jeffry Wyatville, who at length linked his work with that of Nash at Royal Lodge, and whose saloon is the principal reception-room there today.

John Nash reached his mid-forties before gaining a hint of the unsuspected possibilities of royal patronage. A short, stubby, bullet-headed John Bull of a man, with a humorous Cockney mouth and impudent, ironic eyebrows, he returned to London, having designed prisons and villas and obscure little market halls, and formed among other business associations an arrangement with Humphrey Repton, then establishing success as a landscape gardener. Whenever Repton's contrived landscaping demanded a pavilion or a cottage to improve a prospect, or even the entire refacing of a mansion to bring it into classical style, Nash obliged his client at $7\frac{1}{2}$ per cent.

In 1797 Repton undertook to provide a conservatory in the gardens of the Palladian "marine pavilion" at Brighton, which Henry Holland, of Claremont fame, had built ten years earlier for the Prince of Wales, the future George IV. Nash not only supplied the designs but also astutely submitted his drawings to the Royal Academy, correctly anticipating that its members would find it hard to reject a royal commission, and his designs were exhibited the following year. Nothing immediately came of this success, except that artistic recognition set him in high romantic mood and he proposed marriage to a coal-merchant's attractive daughter.

Mary Anne Bradley was twenty-five years old to the bridegroom's forty-six. Possibly Nash was then a widower, for the murky whispers of an earlier wife grow faint and dim. Even murkier whispers were to centre, however, around the new Mrs. Nash; and if, as some have supposed, she was one of the "most lovely girls" whom secretaries procured for the Prince of Wales and smuggled into Carlton House, one can hardly expect the dalliance to be proved by documentary evidence. Although her father had also been bankrupt, Mary Anne mysteriously had money of her own. But it was not his marriage to a pretty and well-to-do young woman that hastened John Nash's road to Royal Lodge. The flicker of his conservatory success disappeared into the limbo of time and for nearly eight years more he continued his cottages and houses and rustic details. What finally did the trick was a cowshed.

Through his Repton connections, Nash designed a thatched *cottage orné* for Sir Charles Taylor at Hollycombe, Liphook. The eccentric exterior with its pointed Strawberry Hill casements and fantastic porch, might well have been cribbed from a dream villa pictured in an album called *Nutshells* some years earlier: but the interior provided an elegant little circular sitting-room, with alcoves and bookcases, of the purest Nash charm. Sir Charles was evidently delighted and he had a knack of moving mountains for those who had pleased him. He enjoyed, too, a facility for winning prizes in the national lottery, including on one occasion the top prize of £20,000. When relatives once sought his advice on what to do with a small legacy, he recommended "Put it in the lottery with me," and a few weeks later placed £500 winnings in their hands.

One must say that it looked suspiciously like jobbery, and Taylor was on the fringe of the Fox-Sheridan Whig coterie who at that time, alert for the profits of a Regency, were among the Prince of Wales' closest friends. Both Fox and Sheridan often stayed with Taylor's friend and neighbour, Lord

Robert Spencer, at Woolbeding, and Nash readily obliged Mr. Fox's friend by designing a cow-house and then a wooden bridge to be built across the river Rother in his grounds. This was in the years 1802–03 when the busy Mr. Nash's commissions included innumerable cottages, an ornamental druidical temple and a brewhouse and, in the interweaving of fate, some work at Whippingham Church, where Humbert, the Sandringham architect, was to begin his career of royal favour precisely fifty years later.

In 1806, by a stroke of great good fortune for Nash, Lord Robert Spencer became Chief Commissioner of Woods and Forests, a post he held for less than a year. But this brief tenure was sufficient for him to appoint John Nash as architect to the department, and although the post offered only £200 a year, Nash had an inkling of its golden opportunities. He could pass to his assistant, Mr. Morgan, such unexciting tasks as repairs for the Duke of Kent's apartments at Hampton Court or the Duke of Clarence's house at Bushy and play a waiting game, and we hear of nothing eventful in his government practice until, in 1811, on the eve of his sixtieth year, Nash was one of four official architects instructed to prepare plans for improving Marylebone Park, the future Regent's Park.

II

George, Prince of Wales, became Regent in February 1811. In that month, the old King George III, mad and nearly blind, was holding jovial conversations with an unseen Henry VIII and Cardinal Wolsey in his guarded northern rooms in Windsor Castle and authoritatively warning his attendants that all human marriages were dissolved. In that month, too, Nash was busy with a workhouse in the Isle of Wight and with Blaise Hamlet, a Bristol banker's commission for a group of romantic cottages on his Somerset estate. In October, we hear of the Regent's pleasure with the "magnificent plan" for the London park, and the terraces and houses encircling it. "It will quite eclipse Napoleon," he had remarked, with some naivety.

It was some years since the Prince had indulged in any personal architectural dissipations. He enjoyed the splurge of his Regency Accession fete at Carlton House — ostensibly to honour the King's birthday — when the carriages of two thousand guests blocked the streets for a mile around. At the then not unusual hour of 2.30 a.m. supper was set before the principal guests on a table two hundred feet long, the meal enlivened by the sight of fish swimming, "or dead and dying" in a cooling stream that meandered on the tabletop between banks of green moss, flowers and silver ornaments. But little enough had been spent on the structure of Carlton House itself for six or seven years and little had changed during that time at Brighton Pavilion.

In that first Regency year the Prince bought many Sandby pictures from Colnaghi's, collecting together drawings dispersed at the auction of Paul Sandby's possessions, and apparently they lit a new flame of enthusiasm for the Windsor scene. The Prince Regent had shuddered at the King's asylum and he had no wish to disturb his mother, Queen Charlotte, or his five spinster sisters. But Cumberland Lodge was vacant, though in disrepair. The Prince Regent's large eyes fell on it, he sought the report of his architect of Woods and Forests and with an audacious optimism that precisely met the Regent's mood Nash suggested that the cost of reconditioning could be met by selling the "top and lop" of the Windsor Forest trees.

Moreover, Mr. Joseph Frost had come to the end of his tether as superintendent of the Windsor farms; and his house, too, the former Lower Lodge or Deputy Ranger's Lodge, could be expediently remodelled — Nash suggested — as a temporary pied-à-terre for the Prince Regent while the repairs of Cumberland Lodge were carried on. With a trivial rearrangement of the floor plan and the introduction of a new staircase for greater convenience, Nash estimated that the works would cost £2,750.

On November 4th, 1812, the Treasury accepted with alacrity a figure they may have found surprisingly low. The shock came a year later when second thoughts showed that all the twigs and loppings of Windsor Forest could not by any means furnish sufficient funds for the renovations of rambling Cumberland Lodge, an expense which the Prince Regent "could have no wish to ask the public to pay." Instead, the ingenious Nash took fresh instructions from the Prince and advised the Treasury that further additions to the cottage would be necessary in order that "His Royal Highness's household might be received." The additional cost would be £13,250.

The only "supplementary" to this, Nash made it appear, would be the cost of chimneypieces for the principal rooms, of a cast-iron conservatory to screen the service quarters and of provision for sinking a deeper well. Remembering the thousands of pounds lavished on the conservatory at Carlton House, which turned out to be fashioned like a soaring Gothic cathedral with a nave and two aisles and windows of stained glass, the Treasury Commissioners should have been forewarned. Thomas Sandby would have stirred in his grave in Windsor churchyard could he have known that his home was one day to receive twenty-nine marble chimneypieces at an average fifty guineas apiece and that the entrance hall and corridor would be paved by some fifty square yards of Portland stone. The Deputy Ranger's Lodge was to disappear into Royal Lodge like Jonah in the whale. The successor to his humble cattle-yard well was ultimately to resemble a mining operation sunk to a depth of 360 feet, and the residues of his own cesspit were one day to upset the whole extravagant scheme.

Within seven days of Nash's new estimate, the Prime Minister was also directly informed that a new road across Windsor Park would be necessary, because the previous road immediately past the door of the cottage transgressed royal privacy. This was to cost £4,404; and from the moment that this was agreed the totals all steadily escalated, and the costs were to run on for nearly twenty years.

The Prince Regent made a feint of looking for less burdensome quarters. There is a tradition that he considered the purchase of Park Place, Henley; and it is said that the Prince admired the rich, medieval half-timbered effect of Ockwells Manor, Maidenhead, but no doubt it was only to ask Nash to bear its romantic elevations in mind. The everlasting plans for improvements at Brighton Pavilion were temporarily forgotten, and the spendthrift magnificences of Carlton House occasioned no public concern for the time being. The Regent had set his heart on realising all the architectural daydreams that gathered around his "Cottage."

In April 1814, England blazed with the flags and illuminations of premature rejoicing of Napoleon's abdication, and the Prince Regent basked not ungratefully in Wellington's reflected glory. "Enjoy the triumph now, Prince of the Mighty Isle," sang the Poet Laureate, Southey, and amid the bells of rejoicing, Nash judiciously submitted his accounts to the Treasury. A total of £1,471 was now due for the marble fireplaces, with £2,733 for the conservatory and a matter of £638 for the well. The treasurers of an exultant nation not only passed the accounts but allowed £1,717 for the enlargement and conversion of the original east drawing-room, and £2,429 for additional offices. These, on examination of Mr. Nash's smooth and tidy script, could be found to include a new servants hall, meat and game larders, a storeroom for the masterpieces of spun sugar with which the Prince Regent liked to decorate his table and sundry other items unexpectedly not covered in the £13,250 for the household.

Flushed with a season of receptions, banquets, fireworks, thanksgiving services, grand Turtle Feasts and cavalry reviews, the Prince Regent drove his mother, the Queen, and his two sisters, Princess Elizabeth and Princess Mary, over from Windsor to view the cottage, one August afternoon. "We all talk of nothing else but your kindness and all those I have seen are full of gratitude and delight with your manners and great good nature," Princess Mary wrote to her brother at about this time.

It made a pleasant family occasion, driving down the Long Walk in an open carriage, with the favourite brother showing off his newest plaything; and yet the Prince could rarely visit a building site without his ardent imagination leaping ahead to the further improvements. Perhaps kind-hearted Princess Mary suggested that her mother might like a glass of cool milk, and there was no longer a dairy and as yet no icehouse. If a cart rattled by while they were inspecting the new rooms, the Prince's acute ear noticed every sound. If one of the sisters paused at the dining-room window, her host immediately realised that the windowsill formed an incumbrance, barring her access to the garden. Walking through the prettily papered bedrooms, the Prince noted that the voices of distant workmen could be heard occasionally through a closed door.

Mr. Nash was summoned for fresh instructions. His Royal Highness required a thatched-roofed icehouse, with suitable drainage. There was to be a dairy, also thatched, built perhaps within a rotunda formed by the rustic columns of trees. A back road was necessary to the offices so that wagons need not pass the front of the house. The windows of the dining-room and drawing-room should be lowered to the floor in the French style. Baize doors to diminish noise and disturbance were to be provided to all bedrooms and principal rooms and a service door should be formed beneath the staircase "to bring in dinner." Was there anything that the princely home-planner had forgotten or overlooked? Spending two nights at Windsor Castle in September, the Prince again drove the Queen and his two sisters to the Cottage, and perhaps it was on this occasion that he discovered the housekeeper would need an additional room and the entire question of service accommodation came up afresh for reconsideration.

The Prince visited Cumberland Lodge with a new view to its use as a service appendage to his own residence, and discussed with Nash the prospect of using some of the better rooms for his guests. Looking sharply into odd corners, the royal eye discovered premature disrepair. It was only five years since the death of the Duchess of Cumberland, she who had once seemed "a coquette beyond measure," and already a garden temple lay in ruins and the house itself, it was noted, seemed "endangered by removing the King's bookcases which supported the upper wall."

So Cumberland Lodge, shunned on account of expense only three years earlier, was now entered in the Prince Regent's further proper requirements for guests and domestic staff; and Nash estimated £286 for a new laundry and wash-house, £331 for a smith's forge "to plan furnished by the Carlton House farrier" and additional provision for new cow-sheds. At the Cottage, too, an extra £656 was required for enlarging the conservatory with a boarded floor to correspond with the existing work. A precise £490 was also to be allowed for a rustic porch. But as if to mollify the Treasury Nash added soothingly that this sum would also allow for "a circular rustic temple, with windows, shutters, linings, etc., and the porch ceiling to be lined with the rustic parts of trees."

The discreet Nash thought it tactful not to reveal that the estimates did not include his own fees for supervision, or that extras awaited accounting to the tune of £5,234. The Prince Regent's architectural finances were in such an inextricable state of magnitude, mystery and muddle that the House of Commons grew alarmed. The £17,000 bill for furnishing provoked a full-dress debate to which Lord Castlereagh could only lamely reply that the Cottage "might be called a cottage, because it was thatched, but the fact was that, though not a residence for a Monarch, it was a very comfortable one for a family, and the only one of which the Prince could make use when he visited Windsor."

III

John Nash equably rode out the storm. He may not have been sufficiently detached to recognise the outraged disappointment in the tone of Whig criticism, but his naive Cockney philosophy gave him assurance that one was safe on the royal side. The Whig politicians had, in fact, expected everything from the Prince except strength. As Roger Fulford has said, "When it dawned on the Whigs, in February, 1812, that after all the years of their attachment to the Prince they were not to achieve office through him, they turned on him with a frenzied ferocity unrivalled in English politics. The rewards of public life, official residences, pensions, the deference of Government servants, the distribution of blue and scarlet ribbons, of glittering orders … were snatched away from them indefinitely." The campaign of hatred outlasted the Prince's lifetime, and the Whig leader, Lord Holland, Fox's nephew, confessed long afterwards, "We all incurred the guilt, if not the odium, of charging His Royal Highness with ingratitude and perfidy. We all encouraged every species of satire against him and his mistress."

Betrayed by old friends, deprived of reliable new ones by his notorious distaste of many of the Tories in government, the Prince sorely needed trustworthy men around him, and Nash emerged at this point as one of the men of the moment. As early as July 1812, when Nash had little to commend him other than his triumphal plans for Regent's Park, the Prince heard that he was on dining terms with Sir Samuel Romilly, the Solicitor-General, and flatteringly suggested that Nash might convey a delicate message.

Romilly was one of the most distinguished lawyers of the day and the Prince felt anxiety on the mischief that his estranged and scandalous wife, Princess Caroline, might cause if enmeshed in a Whig plot. "Little Mr. Nash" obligingly trotted back and forth. He had the ability to paint the Prince's need for private counsel in colours larger than life, and Romilly in turn, on making a casual observation, was amazed to find it interpreted as "advice" to be followed with "attention and respect." Subsequently the Solicitor-General found himself at dinner at Nash's house in Dover Street with Lord Yarmouth, the son of the Prince's sultana, Lady Hertford. Though nothing came of this exercise in intrigue, the Prince Regent had convincing evidence that the reliable Nash had done his best.

There had not yet been time to develop the love-hate relationship of artist and patron, or of architect and client, that occurs in a liaison over-prolonged. For the moment all was honey, the clear honey of the Prince's charm and the thicker grocer's variety which Nash knew, none better, how to spread like his butter on bread. Only a month after the Romilly dinner, Nash's chief superior in office, the architect James Wyatt, Surveyor-General of the Board of Works, was involved in a road accident and killed when his coach and four, travelling at speed, encountered a post-chaise hurtling from the opposite direction. In the scramble for preferment, Wyatt's son, Philip, rushed to the Prince Regent at three in the morning to break the news and, possibly maudlin drunk at that hour, the Prince was able to shed facile tears but rewarded him in no other way. Another Wyatt, nephew Jeffry, penned fifteen letters zealously soliciting influence. John Nash made no move whatever, except perhaps to attend Wyatt's funeral in Westminster Abbey, yet within the week, by direct command of the Prince Regent, he was appointed to the modified post of Deputy Surveyor-General over the heads of all rivals.

The Prince justifiably recognised merit. Nash alone suggested that a set of basement rooms at Carlton House could be transformed, owing to the sloping ground, into a string of dazzling reception-rooms overlooking the garden. Moreover, Nash was a master of such swift organisation that the rooms were ready, dining-room, drawing-room, anterooms, glistening with gold on mouldings and ornaments, completely furnished, in time to form a rich background for the great fete in honour of Wellington in 1814. And this was only a background. To the Prince Regent's considerable satisfaction Nash also designed an immense polygon pavilion in the grounds, firmly built of brick with a leaded roof, the interior draped with white muslin decorated with mirrors, an artful touch of reflection to please the visiting emperors and kings. For the people, too, Nash designed a Chinese bridge and pagoda and it was no fault of the architect that when the pagoda accidentally burst into flames amid the fireworks and toppled into the lake, two trespassers who had climbed to the top suffered the curious fate of being both burned alive or drowned.

Then, in addition, the fertile Nash obligingly turned his mind to the Brighton Pavilion. This he first visited with Bloomfield, the Prince's aide, in January 1815, and promptly began enlarging, renovating and altering in a process that continued, whether he stood in favour or disfavour, for the next eight years. As a telling argument for awarding him the rich plum of the Pavilion, Nash was able to tell Bloomfield the heartening news that the bill for the attendance of masons, plumbers, glaziers, painters and other artisans at the Windsor cottage in 1813 and 1814 came to £27,064, and that this was only £2,076 more than the unrevised estimates.

IV

The Prince Regent took occupation of his Cottage early in the summer of 1815, in Ascot Week, when he slept there for the first time and billeted a large party of extra guests at Cumberland Lodge. His delight in his country home would have been unmarred by the faintest shadow if he could have known that within a matter of days the Battle of Waterloo would have been fought and won. Not that the menace of Bonaparte could sully the Prince's inexhaustible pleasure in regaling his friends with novelty. One can imagine the bowers of blossom, the orchestra in the conservatory, the animating sight and sound, "the kettledrums and cymbals, the glitter of spangles and finery, of dress and furniture" that had enchanted one witness of the Prince Regent's seventh heaven at Carlton House. But instead of sumptuous and overpowering metropolitan richness, the visitor was now enchanted by the perfections of Nature and the comfort and elegance of a Jane Austen cottage, allied to spaciousness and princely style.

In later days, the gossiping and ever-curious world was to glimpse only an immense array of chimneys, as many as thirty, set on rooftops far behind a picket fence, a realm secretive in its thicket as the chateau of the sleeping princess. The sturdy and determined William Cobbett got no farther than one of "the rustic entrance lodges, constructed with boles of oak trees, fixed together in the Swiss manner." But with the freedom of the imagination we are at liberty to enter in, past the high fence and the gate, past the old cottage of the Keeper of the King's Drive (Charles II), down the quarter-mile entrance drive through the trimmed and in part new-planted wood. There is a special pleasure in reconstructing a vanished scene, and the whole of the Cottage that Nash built, except perhaps some part of the cellar, was all swept away in the 1850's, with nothing remaining save the casual phrases of letters and journals, the dull costings of builder's estimates and a few, surprisingly few, sketches to enable us to bring the Prince Regent's home back to life.

Nearing the house the forest of chimneys was lost in the trees and in the semi-circular forecourt Nash had created an illusion of a small cottage by hiding everything except the narrow entrance front behind a screen of shrubs and trees. The visitor on arrival saw only two cream stucco gables projected below the thatched roof while a wide Gothic entrance porch of mellowed timber nestled between them, wreathed in honeysuckle and clematis. Each gable thrust forward on the ground floor a tall bay window, mullioned and leaded, and bonneted with thatch, while demure lace curtains graced the tiny casement windows just above.

It could have been a remote Norfolk parsonage, but for the fondness of peacocks to perch on the tall rustic fence that curved away to the left, and no parson could have afforded the "ornamental wicker basket fifty feet in diameter, of wicker painted green, filled with mould" which had cost £97 and brightened the middle of the forecourt with its abundant flowers. A pair of sumptuous wrought-iron standard lamps, crown-topped, further graced the dark wooden entrance porch. The visitor alighted into a semicircle of cottage flowers and, beyond the inner doors, the paved entrance hall was spacious, cool and dark.

This effect, too, was no doubt deliberate and contrived. Room had been found for a stone staircase with balustrades of ornamental ironwork, and yet a hint of the Sandby ground-plan still lingered in the corridor that ran southward through the house towards the garden. The northern entrance hall, we know, was embellished by "fourteen chairs in the Oriental taste," probably sisters to the flamboyant lacquered chairs of the northern corridors at Brighton rather than a set of carved Chinese Chippendale. To the left opened a small reception-room, and its counterpart on the right of the entrance hall would have served best as the pages' room. These two were the bay-windowed northern rooms overlooking the forecourt. But, cloaked with the invisibility of time travellers, we can steal down the corridor and discover that the next room on the left leads into the eating-room and so, one room opening into another, to the full suite of royal apartments. Here, from the Sandbys' old south-east sitting-room, the venturesome Nash had removed a fireplace, supporting the chimney shaft above with unseen iron girders, to create space for folding doors that opened into an entirely new wing.

The modern eye would note that none of the ground floor windows opened direct into sunlight. Each was screened by the heavy thatch of the verandah, with its rose-wreathed supporting pergola, that ran east and south round the house. The "bright effulgence of the luminous orb" was not allowed to fade the carpets, a domestic precaution which may have also enhanced the colour and clarity of the pretty wallpapers that invited admiration in every room. Nash's estimates whisper the shanty impermanence of the structure: many of the inner walls were mere partitions "panelled in deal and wallpapered." But to the random guest one could not "imagine anything more beautiful... The rooms are low but light, elegantly and not gorgeously furnished, many admirable pictures..."

The effect expressed the owner's plainer tastes, though probably some of the £17,000 spent on furnishing was expressed in the boule cabinets and grandiose French commodes that turned up at Windsor Castle in the great furniture reshuffle of 1866. The two corner cupboards of red, black and gold European lacquer by the French maître Vanrisamburgh, certainly stood in one of the rooms. Today these are the choice *encoignure* of the present Royal Collection. At a later date, a carved armchair formed their uneasy companion. Carved from the elm tree that stood in the centre of the British lines on the field of Waterloo, the owner was apt to surprise guests by regarding it proudly and asserting, "I was there!"

The domestic scale of the twelve reception-rooms would have suggested small pictures, and probably the Cottage sheltered some of the Dutch paintings which Lord Yarmouth at Christie's and elsewhere bought on behalf of the Prince in

1814, the smaller Teniers, the Wouwermans and Van Mieris and other "little masters." At a time when the furnishing of the Cottage occupied his thoughts, the Prince Regent also acquired Wilkie's "Penny Wedding" and "Blind Man's Buff" and other homely *genre* pictures that denoted his patronage of British artists. His earlier purchases from George Stubbs and William Birds may also have found their way to his country rooms, and the Prince would not have missed the appropriate touch of placing some of his Sandby drawings on view in what could still, reminiscently, rank as the Sandby home. One pictures them flanking the marble fireplaces in one or other of the seventeen bedrooms. The handsome Lady Hertford — whether her relationship with the Prince Regent was platonic or no — needed no better reminder of her admirer's future than a picture of Windsor Castle, not too far from her bedside.

The dignified Marchioness of Hertford no doubt still filled a role as hostess more than guest, though her star was past its zenith. The Emperor of Russia had thought her "mighty old" when introduced to her two years earlier, yet in reality she was only two years older than the Prince Regent, who was fifty-three, the natural russet of her coiffure closely according with his own new flattering wig of short brown curls. For more than four years now, she had completely supplanted Mrs. Fitzherbert in intimacy, influence and affection. Her husband was Lord Chamberlain and thus technically head of the Prince's household. Her red-whiskered son, Lord Yarmouth, was one of the Prince's closest friends and probably his best-heeded artistic adviser.

They all made a happy family in that first Ascot week at the royal Cottage. We can hear the buzz of conversation in the evening beneath the trellised green-painted cast-iron pilasters of the conservatory, as the company strolled back and forth on a new floor, yet another, of "hexagonal brick tiles," while the orchestra played ensconced amid foliage in its own latticed temple.

All was delightful and probably the proud owner did not discover until an autumn visit that the chimneys smoked. Thanks to an Ackermann print, we can stand back on the lawns and gaze at the house, the conservatory to the left like a Regency birdcage, the lattice windows of a line of bedrooms twinkling beneath the thatched dormers, and the lines of offending chimneys rising through the thatch. Nash had an immediate answer by fitting at least nine with pots or "smoke preventers," but one cannot resist a shudder at the thought of the regiment of chimneys belching smoke and sparks downward across the thatched roofs. It was a miracle that the Prince Regent was not burned in his bed.

8: THE ROYAL LODGE

I

Among the sweets of office for Mr. Nash was an airy suite of rooms at Cumberland Lodge which he treated so much as his own that the Board of Works rebuked him early in 1816 for cutting a doorway without official authorisation. Nash disliked to put a foot wrong and he invited Sir Samuel Romilly to stay with him at Cumberland Lodge at Whitsun, in the congenial company of Benjamin West, the painter, and other guests, for a weekend affording an opportunity to discuss the paradox of a government department that quarrelled with its chieftain, with himself, indeed, as Deputy Surveyor-General. Nash was able to offer his guests more than princely comfort, for the great house had been sumptuously equipped with part of £35,000 worth of furniture bought for the reception of the Allied Sovereigns in 1814. Like any businessman, the architect combined business with pleasure. Some of his draughtsmen worked at Cumberland Lodge from time to time, and he had ledgers to prove that two of his staff had been busy there on the Prince Regent's concerns that very March, a month in which Nash submitted a £5,234 bill for extras. But the need for the Solicitor-General's advice was more acute, for Nash regarded himself as working privately as architect to the Prince Regent and now faced the acute diplomatic difficulty that the Department looked askance at his fees.

If the Treasury accountants imagined that his services for the royal Cottage, Carlton House and the Pavilion were included within his official salary of £200 a year (plus a shilling a mile travelling allowance) they were to be disillusioned. In August,

Nash submitted his bills for £30,783 2s. 2½d. and to the punctilious last ha'penny were added his architect's charges. The total of this interesting item has disappeared but the Public Record Office preserves Nash's letter of August 24th in response to Treasury argument. He considered himself employed at the Cottage, he wrote, as at Carlton House, "namely, as architect of the Prince Regent and in the same way as I am employed by other individuals: the duties I performed were precisely the same. I made the designs and all the detailed drawings for carrying the works into execution, surveyed the work from time to time in its progress and measured and made out the tradesmen's bills — with the difference only that in building the cottage I have much additional trouble with the accounts, there being no clerk of the works. With regard to my selection as a surveyor of the Office of Works I am joined with Mr. Morgan in that office and we both of us considered the cottage as a distinct work done by men for the sovereign in his private house and as His Royal Highness's private architect."

The outcome of this controversy is not on record, but that it reached a favourable conclusion for Nash may be deduced from his continued services to his royal client. In September the Treasury expressed satisfaction with his bills, except for £3,102 still due to various tradesmen. Public and private, the Regent's debts were notorious, and it may be amusing at this remove of time to delve into the affairs of at least one of these tradesmen who did not always rely on Mr. Nash's finesse to extract his money.

A Sunningdale builder and bricklayer named Charles Dolby, for example, had already drawn lump payments of £2,876 and £2,539 and was apparently still owed a large sum, but this disability did not prevent him from competing in vaguely-worded tenders to build a wall round the Lodge at £15 10s. a rod. Mr. Dolby feared that he might be at a disadvantage against his rivals. "Having always done the bricklayers' work at the Lodge," he urged, in a covering letter, "I have made my contract with but little if any profit. If it should not be the lowest, I hope you will not deem me presumptuous in wishing to have the contract, when it is considered that I am a great sufferer by the long credit."

He was indeed awarded the contract but there were difficulties six months later, in April 1817, when the Prince Regent found the wall unfinished. Mr. Dolby had taken his men away in the depth of winter. "At the time," he explained to the Office of Works, "I had but few bricks in my yard fit for the job," and he added, cheekily, "and I am sorry to add that I had not the means to purchase any, owing to being kept out of money so long due to me, the arrears for which I petitioned the Lords of the Treasury ten months since."

By return post this brought such a rocket from Colonel Stephenson, of the Office of Works, that the poor man had to recant. "I throw myself on your mercy," he wrote, in an agony of terror. The rain had spoiled thousands of bricks, Mr. Nash had seen no objection to completing the work in the Spring and so on.

At the end of 1818 the contractor was still tendering his bill, pointing out that the work had been finished for sixteen months. The Office of Works consulted Nash, and the architect demurred that this or that had not been authorised. Seventy-two rods at £15 10s. came to £1,116 but there were inevitable extras for drains, digging the ground and cutting to waste, and finally Nash agreed that the heavy rains had caused a quagmire, rendering estimates difficult, and he agreed the bill for the wall at £1,733. One cannot tell whether Dolby then received his money. As late as 1822, the Treasury ordered that debts of £12,000 outstanding to various tradesmen should be defrayed by the sale of timber in the Great Park "which may be felled without any injury to the beauty thereof."

In referring to the Lodge, Mr. Dolby evidently still had in mind the Deputy Ranger's Lodge, for the name "Royal Lodge" was then reserved for a house at Weymouth owned by George III, and the name was otherwise unknown at Windsor until after the Regent succeeded as King George IV in 1820. Contemporaries referred to it as the Regent's Cottage when, safe within the enclosure of Mr. Dolby's completed walls, the Prince Regent's sister, Princess Elizabeth, spent her honeymoon there with the Hereditary Prince of Hesse-Homburg in April 1818. The sprightly commentators of twentieth-century royal romances might have found it difficult to garnish this event with their customary confections. "An uglier hound, with a snout buried in hair, I never saw," wrote one of the Duke of Buckingham's correspondents. Jerningham also reported, "They immersed him several times in a warm bath to make him a little clean," and the chivalrous Sir William Fremantle added, "It is impossible to describe the monster … vulgar-looking, breath and hide a compound between tobacco and garlick. What can have induced her nobody can guess."

To the Regent's middle-aged sister, however, the reviled creature became "my beloved husband" and she was grief-stricken when he died eleven years later. "No woman was ever more happy than I was," she wrote to Sir William Knighton. Admittedly, the honeymoon began badly when her bridegroom was sick during the drive to the Cottage "from being unused to a close carriage." The bride's trousseau included gowns of "white satin, Pomona green satin, lilac-and-white striped satin and white kerseymere" but she can have found scant opportunity to display them. The bridegroom, we are told, was not so much bored at the cottage as he expected, "having passed all his time in his dressing-gown and slippers smoking in the Conservatory."

The smell that hung about the place, moreover, was not that of the bridegroom. Even Mr. Nash was hard put to it to explain the noxious, yellowish, fast-spreading tentacles of dry rot that appeared in the cupboards and skirtings of all the main rooms.

II

The lintels over the folding-doors that perilously carried the weight of a chimney-stack were first found to be affected by decay in 1817. "I fear it has spread in the floor above. In fact, I do not know where it will end," reported a timorous surveyor. Nash had the floors temporarily re-laid and the wall panels hurriedly papered over in order that the Regent could use the house for the Ascot races, and after the royal guests had politely endured the stench during the festivities of Ascot week, he made a more searching investigation. To save time, money and materials, much of the Cottage had been built on the Sandby foundations without too close an inspection, but Nash made a point of never being at fault, difficult as it was to describe the harsh realities underlying the royal elegance and refinement. "An old drain and cesspool a little below the surface of the ground under the parlour of the Old House was not known to exist," he reported, "till in tracing the process of the present mischief it was discovered. It was there it originated," mentioned Mr. Nash guardedly, and not "in the New Work." But in case this seemed insufficient explanation of the fungus "making so destructive a progress in the building," he conceded that excavations under the smaller drawing-room had also revealed "an old drain full of filth: the

131

drains having fallen in, it spreads under the floors…"

Since the Prince Regent at this time was employing Nash chiefly at Brighton, he may not have been aware of the full extent of the trouble or, at all events, he was readily placated. In his absence, the floors of "the eating-room, both drawing-rooms and the back gallery as far westwards as the arched cellar" were taken up. It was more difficult for Nash to conceal from his indulgent patron that some part of the roofing thatch had already decayed "not having been made of reed" and had to be replaced by slates at a cost of £740.

III

The old King George III died in January 1820, when the Regent was also seriously ill at Brighton, but on the day after the unparalleled splendour of his coronation the new King George IV withdrew to the King's Cottage, as it now became known, for ten days. Once again there were new additions and alterations to enjoy, a new suite of guest apartments, a large dining-room and billiard-room and "a covered walk, in a serpentine form, leading from the Conservatory into the grounds for the convenience of His Majesty and his visitors during wet weather." This luxurious avenue contained "all the rare shrubs, flowers and creeping plants" that could be collected. Did the blossoms recall romantic moments with Mrs. Fitzherbert or Lady Hertford? The first was in embittered retirement, the old doting friendship with the second had cooled, and the King strutted sedately through his arbours with a new love, the "large-balconied" Lady Conyngham, a plump charmer of fifty-two, now installed in the Cottage *en famille* with her husband and their five grown-up children.

For added diversion another small menagerie invited inspection at Sandpit Gate, but the animals were no stranger than the royal menage. Lord Conyngham was appointed Lord Steward of the Household and Lady Conyngham adorned with the title of Lady Steward. Croker, the diarist, records that a ribald nation dubbed her the Vice Queen, and caricaturists made full play with the harmonies of her phenomenal bosom and the King's spheroid stomach. Watching them at a ball at Carlton House with eyes screwed up in disgust, Mrs. Arbuthnot considered that the King made "a complete fool of himself all evening with Lady Conyngham," especially when he at last shut himself up in a room with her and placed a page to guard the door. But there were no priggish, spying eyes at the Cottage. Wellington noted sharply that the two drove down there alone together "tête-à-tête in the carriage," but the Iron Duke was so often wrong about the royal love affairs. The King ended a characteristic letter, "I hasten to inhale as much as I can of the pure air of this delightful spot," and the dull domestic evenings of music, patience and rereading Jane Austen were hardly the "pagan disports" of popular imagination.

Dorothea de Lieven, the Russian ambassador's wife, recorded a wet weekend when field mice came in from the garden and ran about the floors. "After dinner the piano. After the piano ecarte, and at twelve to bed." The following evening passed with "fourteen games of ecarte and thirty-three games of patience." One may suppose that the friendship with Lady Conyngham was platonic, and made to appear otherwise by the King's mawkish and over-demonstrative sentimentality. He told Madame de Lieven that he did nothing from morning to night but think what he could do to please Lady Conyngham and make her happy, and de Lieven reported acidly to Prince Metternich that the source of this rapture could dispense with sentiment but "she can't do without diamonds." Yet Lieven saw that Lady Conyngham was also a very religious woman, her otherwise vapid mind "being occupied with religious questions." Lady Conyngham would never play cards on Sundays, and it is amusing to find that what she wanted above all from the King at this stage was a convenient chapel.

She evidently disliked the early-morning turnout to St. George's Chapel, Windsor, and the drive to the private chapel at Cumberland Lodge was no better. In cold weather she persuaded the King to keep to the house, and a service would then be held in the Cottage dining-room. In making an attempt to regularise this unsanctified place of worship, the King ordered that the pulpit should be brought down from Cumberland Lodge. The Office of Works inadvertently countermanded this direct command and the Prime Minister had to intervene to soften the King's wrath. "The incident which has given offence to Your Majesty must have arisen from some misunderstanding," he wrote humbly, and there was generally hell to pay.

The incident interests us, for the new chapel was the first work of Jeffry Wyatt in the Royal Lodge scene. Head of a contracting firm of carpenters, a stumpy man of "inelegant personal form, redeemed by liveliness of expression," as Farington tells us, he had aspired to fill his uncle's post of Surveyor-General ten years earlier only to see the vacant chair filled by Nash, and now in direct competition with Nash he had his estimates and plans victoriously chosen for the restoration and Gothic refurbishing of Windsor Castle. Nash at this point disappears from the Windsor scene, though still with honours for he was awarded the alternative plum of the works at Buckingham Palace. Wyatt deployed five hundred workmen at Windsor Castle, a force providing an ample labour pool for extra work at the Cottage. The King wanted more bookcases in his library and a projecting bow window to lend space to a small adjoining room. The chapel, too, had to be formed "within an old building," presumably an old porter's lodge, for a new porter's lodge was also built at this time.

In August, 1824, the King drove up from the Cottage to Windsor Town to lay the foundation stone of a new gateway to the renovated Castle, and Wyatt asked permission to change his name to Wyatville, to distinguish himself from his relatives. "Veal or mutton, call yourself what you like," the King told the "bustling, vain little man," but presumably this change dropped a pebble into the ever active whirlpools of the King's mind. On March 2nd, 1825, he addressed a letter as from King's Lodge, and on July 15th he used the heading "Royal Lodge." It was reported that on Palm Sunday, March 27th, the King attended Divine Worship "for the first time in the new Chapel in the pleasure grounds adjoining the Royal Lodge," but the term Royal Lodge had also crept into print in October the previous year. The new name was at last definitive.

A covered way of a hundred yards enabled the King and the Conynghams to approach the chapel unseen from the house. The one fault was a step at the King's pew at which he "nearly broke his head" and which Wyatville was required to remedy.

Chaplains were warned by the King's secretary never to preach on "mere moral duties and virtues," the safe course "to keep entirely to doctrinal explanations." The King listened to such sermons "with profound attention" but later on, as Lady Caroline Damer tells us, the royal pew was fitted with a screen so that neither clergyman nor congregation could tell whether His Majesty were present and paying attention or not. Equally unable to see the preacher, the King perhaps gazed at the stained-glass window over the altar which, a sermon in itself, paid regard to the illness of George III and represented the Saviour casting out devils.

The private chapel or church of All Saints was completely rebuilt by Queen Victoria in 1864 and now, at the entrance to Royal Lodge, stone-built and ivy-clad, filled with memorials of the past, it is known as the Royal Chapel, Windsor Great Park. When members of the Royal Family today attend morning service there, their presence is usually notified next morning in the Court Circular, a singular link with the conscience of Lady Conyngham.

IV

As early as 1820 an elephant was kept at the stables of Cumberland Lodge for the entertainment and interest of guests. It was viewed, among other unlikely visitors, by four Red Indian chiefs who were shown these correct elephantine proportions after they had talked to the King on the lawns of his Cottage and enjoyed "the interior of the house, the stables, the animals and the birds." They were three months too soon to view the ostriches sent by the King of Sockatoo from Central Africa, the second batch of their species within a century to face the hazards of the English winter. One of the birds did not last long and when a post-mortem revealed a stomach stuffed with scraps of wood, iron nails and other objects, the cause of death was certified as obesity. Subsequently, not to waste a good bird, a group of professors sat down to sample roast ostrich and pronounced it excellent, more resembling beef than fowl.

In 1825, too, a visitor to Virginia Water found a new Chinese building and a picturesque boathouse in course of building. Wyatville was also responsible for a Fishing Temple, new waterfalls and other works, and by a pleasant chance of timing these were ready for the future Queen Victoria when, as a child of seven the following year, she visited her "Uncle King" with her mother and her half-sister Princess Feodora. Every detail of this unusual outing was still vividly remembered more than forty years later when the Queen jotted down some childhood recollections. "When we arrived at the Royal Lodge, the King took me by the hand, saying 'Give me your little paw.' He was large and gouty, but with a wonderful dignity and charm of manner." The King presented her with the Windsor family Order with his portrait set in diamonds, and Lady Conyngham pinned it to her shoulder. Next day, chancing to see his niece from his phaeton, the King cried jovially "Pop her in!"

"I was greatly pleased and remember that I looked with great respect at the scarlet liveries..." Queen Victoria recollected. "We drove around the nicest part of Virginia Water and stopped at the Fishing Temple. Here was a large barge and everyone went on board and fished, while a band played in another! There were numbers of great people there ... the King paid much attention to my Sister, and some people fancied he might marry her!"

Afterwards, in the Page Whiting's cottage, "the little cottage close by," the Princess naughtily amused herself "by cramming one of Whiting's children, a little girl, with peaches." That evening the conservatory glowed with coloured lamps and the King promised his niece that the band would play anything she pleased: she had only to name it. "Oh Uncle King," she quickly replied, "I should like 'God Save the King'."

The following year, little Princess Victoria's second visit was less successful. An encampment of tents "quite like a house, made into different compartments" had been prepared to regale the guests, but torrential rain damped the picnic. If she then visited the menagerie as she had done the previous year, the Princess was a few days too early to see the famous giraffe, one of the first ever to reach England, which was presented to the King by the Pasha of Egypt and arrived at Royal Lodge in the late summer of 1827. Captured as a calf, strapped to the back of a camel throughout a dreadful six weeks journey across the desert, the poor beast barely survived. A windlass had to be arranged at Windsor to assist its weak and unsteady legs and it died two years later. But with its Arab attendants, it was a briefly enchanting addition to the exotic flavours of the Lodge and the vicinity.

The incentive of the Fishing Temple originated with some Greek statuary, captured from a French frigate, which had lain neglected for years in a courtyard of the British Museum. The King, with Wyatville's help, dreamed them into a miniature Parthenon and with them arrived the columns and capitals which had been brought six or seven years earlier from the ruined Roman city of Leptis Magna as a gift from the Bey of Tripoli. The romantic transplant still defies time on the lakeside of Virginia Water, though some of the Corinthian columns are precariously balanced and others have fallen, but the statues had to be removed, to preserve them from the mutilation administered by the appreciative British public when William IV threw open Windsor Great Park in 1830.

The fragments caused excitement in 1852 when they were unearthed in a garden yard, "statues of Venus, Ceres, Fauns, Satyrs … their heads severed, their arms and legs broken off, their beauty effaced…" Perhaps the garden yard was that of Royal Lodge itself, though we cannot be sure of their ultimate fate. More recently, dismembered stone limbs and a fragment of torso were retrieved from a rubbish dump in the grounds of the Lodge, but these resembled the discarded portions of a group of statuary by the Flemish sculptor Pierre de

Francheville, brought from Hampton Court to Windsor and similarly disinterred at the Lodge in the 1860's, and so the identification of the Queen Mother's "treasure" remains an open question.

With an opulent gilded royal barge, a miniature frigate, the *Victorine*, and other craft, Virginia Water at times had a lovely appearance in those Georgian days. The Culloden guns were brought down to the lakeside from Fort Belvedere to fire a salute on the King's birthday, and in 1827 George IV organised one of his elaborate marquee dinner parties to receive his eldest sister, the dowager Queen of Wurttemberg. "We ladies crossed in an excellent boat to the island, where the old boathouse has been turned into a very pretty building," wrote another sister, the Princess Augusta. "There are six strong Pullers, who belong to the boat, all simply and properly dressed in blue-and-white striped jackets, white trousers and straw hats." With this handsome crew the King and his sisters later "took a delightful row by moonlight."

Another visitor was Sir Walter Scott, who chronicled in his journal his impressions that "the Lodge in the Forest, though ridiculed by connoisseurs, seems to be no bad specimen of a royal retirement... A kind of cottage, too large perhaps for the royal style, but yet so managed that in the walks you only see parts of it at once, and these well composed and grouping with the immense trees." There were only six or seven to dinner and, after leaving table, "excellent music by the royal band, who lay ambushed in a greenhouse... The King made me sit beside him and talked a great deal — too much perhaps..." Dorothea de Lieven mentions, too, that despite "the rarest union of comfort, elegance and magnificence," there were ordinarily only six at dinner. In the more festive atmosphere of Ascot Week, Charles Greville was present at a Jockey Club dinner when thirty sat down. "Nothing can exceed the luxury of the internal arrangements," he noted, although the rooms appeared to him "too low and too small for very large parties." The celebrated Tyrolese dancers made the evening pass off tolerably, although Lady Conyngham looked "bored to death … she never speaks," Greville added, "never appears to have one word to say to the King."

But perhaps Lady Conyngham, as well as Greville, was conscious of oppression and stuffiness in the low rooms. Behind the "unspoiled magnificence" was a familiar faint lurking smell, for dry rot was again gaining hold.

V

From mid-1827 until the end of 1828 Royal Lodge was George IV's only home. Carlton House had been dismantled and was awaiting demolition, and when the King went to town he used only a small suite of rooms at St. James's Palace. Upwards of half-a-million had been spent on Buckingham Palace and yet the place was still unfinished and uninhabitable with hardly a room completed. As great a fortune again had been lavished on Windsor Castle, where the end was only remotely in sight. At Brighton, the Pavilion in the midst of the fast-developing town no longer afforded privacy and the King completely abandoned it after a final visit early in the year. Querulous, gouty, his puffy features now beyond the artifice of cosmeticians, his unwieldy form outraging the skill even of Shea, his favourite tailor, the tricks that time had played on him affronted the monarch's vanity and he withdrew more and more from the eyes of men.

Sir Walter Scott had noted "a sort of reserve which creeps on him daily" and Lord Harcourt, the Ranger of Windsor Park, began to have an anxious time ensuring that the King should

140

never "see a strange face, or even a human being of any kind, within his domain." At the hour when the King was liable to take "the exercise of the phaeton," the park gates were rigorously closed while the park-keepers in their camouflage green livery alertly patrolled every route he might favour. The people heard of him taking his rides, says Huish, with "his favourite outrider Hudson casting his eyes into every brake or thicket to ascertain if some prying, inquisitive intruder, some 'peeping Tom' had not there concealed himself..."

One difficulty was a tower, commonly called the clock-case from some imagined resemblance in its form, which stood just outside the Great Park, rising high above the trees, and afforded a good view of the royal roads near Virginia Water. So satisfying was the view indeed that the proprietor made a charge for admission to a telescope on the roof and run by an old couple, the place became a resort for picnic parties. The King had no recourse but to purchase the tower at the exorbitant price asked and then firmly exclude the public. Long since gone were the days when the poet Shelley could sail paper boats in the lakeside shallows, freighted with halfpennies for the amusement of small boys. No longer could the novelist Thomas Love Peacock bring literary friends this way for a stroll from his house at Englefield Green. Mystery deepened around the eccentric recluse of Windsor, and the more the monarch insisted on privacy the wilder grew the surmise and rumour.

The King was said to ask his page for clothes he had worn years before, and Wyatville's Fishing Temple became enlarged in popular imagination into another expensive palace "of pure and chaste design" to be built like a second Carlton House in the southern recesses of Windsor Park. His sight failing in one eye, the King found the rooms at Royal Lodge becoming "inconveniently dark" and he ordered the verandah roofs to be raised, and the light improved by replacing the sloping slates and thatch with a lead flat. The octagonal tiles in the conservatory became precarious to his crutches and nothing would suit but that it should be entirely refloored with Portland stone. He worried about fire hazards and demanded a new fire engine for which Treasury officials went into a catalepsy of estimates. He sniffed suspiciously at the lavatories and desired that "the watercloset at the foot of the great stairs" should be taken away. He complained irritably to his secretary that no single step was taken to carry his orders into effect. It could not be denied that it took months to complete "a bath adjoining His Majesty's own apartments," and the King demanded that Wyatville should immediately receive "written orders to proceed with all speed."

At last, on December 9th 1828, the King drove over to Windsor to receive the keys of his new apartments in the Castle. With a sense of occasion the architect knelt to present them in a crimson bag and arose Sir Jeffry Wyatville. The King then seems to have taken the opportunity to ventilate his latest idea for the Lodge — a vision of a fine and lofty dining-room — for within the week Sir Jeffry was reported to be asking for "tenders for the new work."

The King was compelled to retreat into the Castle while workmen cleaned the drains at the Lodge, stopped up "all rat holes and vents by which the Smells arise to His Majesty's apartments," and particularly examined all the cupboards and crannies adjoining the drawing-room and conservatory where the smell was "particularly evil." The King's water closet was also to receive particular attention; the "cellars under the drawing-room to be arched over" and the damp and crumbling stack of chimneys at the conservatory entrance to be renewed.

Any modern architect could diagnose a classic case of dry rot, but the Lords of the Treasury approved £7,300 for Wyatville's "additions and alterations" early in 1829.

Some patching-up was effected in time for the King to spend the summer at Royal Lodge, and the poor ailing old creature felt that he was happier there than anywhere, with Lady Conyngham's silent company and the raucous screeching of his pet cockatoo. Charles Greville reported that "the King's mind is quite made up never to live in the Castle … he says it is too public." But the physicians had already forbidden him, in view of his swollen hands, to indulge in his favourite recreation of fishing at Virginia Water, and with the renewed autumn rains the dampness of Royal Lodge became unmistakable. The King removed to Windsor Castle with a regretful glance at Wyatville's plans and the £8,500 estimate for his new dining-room over the basement kitchen.

So much had been planned. So much was incomplete. He had trifled for years with a grandiose scheme to adorn the landscape with an enormous copper equestrian statue of his father on the summit of Snow Hill at the end of the Long Walk. The "Copper Horse" — as it ultimately became known — was in readiness in London, and twelve workmen had signified its hugeness by taking their dinner inside it, but as yet the King had seen only the foundation stone of its pedestal well and truly laid. He returned to Windsor Castle on December 17th 1829, and began driving over to the Lodge in his pony phaeton in March to inspect the improvements, planning to resume residence on June 1st. The last excursion was on April 12th, and that night he had one of the seizures of breathlessness that frightened everyone when he went purple in the face.

His heart was affected and the doctors realised he was nearing his last days. The King knew it too. "The poor cottage!" he said to Sir Robert Peel on May 17th, "I shall never see it again." On the morning of June 26th the servants at Royal Lodge heard that their master was dead.

9: TRANSITIONAL

I

King George IV's younger brother, the Duke of Clarence, was still in bed with his Duchess when the Duke of Wellington came to make a low obeisance to him and announce his accession to the Throne. The new King William IV heard the news in his dressing-gown, much as his niece, Victoria, was to do seven years later, and then murmured that he would return to bed and indeed "wished particularly to do so, having never yet been in bed with a Queen." At Windsor Castle, hundreds of "servants, their families and acquaintance" filed past the corpse of the old King and took their leave by shaking the dead hand, while trespassers already invaded the sacrosanct glades around Royal Lodge. A park-keeper warned the artist, Melville, that His Majesty had issued positive commands against sketching, only to receive the insolent reply that "as the King lay dead in Windsor Castle, was not the command dead also?"

Charles Greville, Clerk-in-Ordinary to the Privy Council, could scarcely contain his curiosity and piled his friends into four carriages to explore all the late King's private drives. He recorded with satisfaction that his party "saw all the penetralia of the late King, whose ghost must have been indignant at seeing us scampering all about his most secret recesses." William IV had directed that all the drives of the park should be thrown open except to carriages, and Lady Sefton specially applied to the King to be allowed to see Virginia Water from her own conveyance. Of this expedition Greville recorded, "They thought it was the Queen coming ... the man on board

145

the little frigate hoisted all the colours and the boatman on the other side got ready the royal barge to take us across." Delighted with the luxury and beauty, the party inspected the communicating tents "forming a very good house, a dining-room, drawing-room, and several other small rooms, very well furnished. Across the water is the fishing-cottage, beautifully ornamented, with one large room and a dressing-room on either side, kitchen-offices, etc., and in a garden full of flowers." The new King was told the story of the clock-case, and rubbed his hands. "A good place for a view, is it? Put an old couple into it and *give* them a telescope!"

There can indeed have been little peace for the unquiet spirit of George IV. The birds and beasts of his menagerie were dispatched to the London Zoo. His wardrobes at Royal Lodge and elsewhere were opened to reveal dirty handkerchiefs, faded nosegays, scores of waistcoats, three hundred whips, every sort of uniform; and these unhappy remnants were sent to auction and the royal pages divided the £15,000 proceeds as their perquisite. Meanwhile, William IV visited Royal Lodge, his large, choleric eyes undeceived by the lick of fresh paint over decaying wood, and he brusquely ordered all the old part to be pulled down. Wyatville was no doubt able to tell this "bluff, good-natured, kind-hearted gentleman" the horrific home truths about the structure that he had kept from King George.

It has become a legend that pious Queen Adelaide persuaded her husband to pull down Royal Lodge because she could not bear to contemplate its scenes of immorality, but the real explanation was less novelettish. Dry rot now infected every part of the old building, save the cast-iron conservatory, and demolition was the only radical cure. The best furnishings were dispersed among the other royal residences and few of the earlier links with Royal Lodge can now be readily identified.

The marble chimney pieces were either transferred to Buckingham Palace or sold in a demolition yard. Within a year of the death of George IV, house-breakers had all but cleared the site, and only the conservatory, the little chapel and a gardener's cottage or two remained, with Sir Jeffry Wyatville's dining-room standing gaunt and new.

Some of the building materials — especially slates, bricks and window frames — were transferred to build a summer retreat for Queen Adelaide in the Home Park, thus demonstrating that the gentle and good-hearted lady did not find the link of sentiment intolerable and judged George IV's peccadilloes no more harshly than her own husband's earlier relations with the actress, Mrs. Jordan. The Queen first used Adelaide Cottage on her thirty-ninth birthday in August 1831, though it must have seemed a little cramped for royal rejoicings. Meanwhile, services were regularly held at the Royal Lodge chapel "for the benefit of the servants of the Park Establishment" and the Queen occasionally visited the abandoned garden during her daily rides, and pondered and planned what might become of the remaining fragments.

The octagonal outline at the end of the conservatory provided the inspiration of a separate pavilion or retiring room. The Octagonal Room that served as foundation to the late Queen Mother's sitting-room was, in fact, Queen Adelaide's contribution to the structure, "fitted up like a tent, the corners taken off by draperies, or open with sofas in the recess — *very pretty*," as one of the Queen's guests, Lady Wharncliffe, described it. "Windows every way, or rather to the view and to the old lawn, the other sides having glass doors."

Apparently the formal inauguration of the Lodge in its new guise was staged for Queen Adelaide's birthday on August 13th, 1833. It was one of those flourishes of genial family hospitality that King William IV so much enjoyed. A royal procession of fifteen carriages set out from the Castle, attended by outriders in scarlet liveries, and a cavalcade of gentlemen of the Household on horseback. At the Lodge a magnificent set of Burmese tents, which the Queen had never seen, were put up as an extra surprise for her, and the dining-room itself was fitted at one end with a huge mirror to double its apparent vista. The fourteen-year-old Princess Victoria and her mother, the Duchess of Kent, were almost certainly among the ninety guests, one of whom — a Miss Clitherow, daughter of one of the Queen's old Bushy neighbours — has left us a charming eyewitness description:

> I never saw anything prettier than the whole scene and the day was lovely. The tents were the most brilliant scarlet ornamented with gold and silver. The hangings, sofas and seats were all of Eastern splendour ... the company was very select, and the morning dresses becoming and elegant. Two bands of music (Guards) played alternately. A guard of honour and numbers of officers were present.
>
> Everybody seemed gay, and in their best fashion. The King and Queen, with about forty guests, dined in the room, about as many more in a long canvas room. The tables had fruit, flowers, ornaments, confectionery, a few pyramids of cold tongue, ham, chicken, and raised pies. Then you had handed to you soups, fish, turtle, venison and every sort of meat. Toasts were given, cannons fired and both bands united in the appropriate national airs. Altogether it was a sort of enchantment...

Less ornate fetes centred around the Fishing Temple, where the "fourteen Oriental seats" from the former hallway of Royal Lodge now filled the central room, not out of place against the hangings of "green chintz sprinkled with marine productions."

The first Lady Wharncliffe was a visitor who remembered the old days, the charades staged before George IV and Lady Conyngham, the orchestras under the coloured lights, and then, one day when out for a drive with the Queen she saw Royal Lodge again with all the nostalgia of things past: "We returned by Cumberland Lodge and the remains of our poor dear *Cottage!* I can't say how unpleasant it was, and I could not help saying to the Queen as we walked thro' the Conservatory how melancholy it was to me. She said nothing, but looked hard at me, with an inquisitive but amiable expression. I did not choose to expatiate, and she did not speak, but she saw there was something she did not understand. The new dining-room was not quite finished by poor George IVth, but is now complete (and where *we* should have dined had he lived another year... The carriage drives up and sets you down at the end of the Conservatory, exactly where the house joined, on the very stage of your charades! I really was quite glad to leave the spot..."

Adelaide's closest confidante in England, the Duchess of Kent, must on the other hand have shared her enjoyment of the Lodge, sufficiently to recount its delights to her brother, the Duke Ernest of Saxe-Coburg. Queen Adelaide and Victoire of Kent were both German-born royalties who had been brides together in 1818 at a double wedding at Kew Palace. The Royal Lodge was a natural objective in their afternoon drives, from Windsor Castle down the Long Walk. On the way they passed Westmacott's statue of George III on his colossal copper steed, firm and safe now on its pedestal, although when first drawn to the spot four years earlier the wagon had sunk into the earth with the weight of its burden. One of the outsize metal legs was snapped in this accident, but a furnace was resourcefully kindled on the spot and repairs effected. The

Queen ordered her coachman to drive round the statue, stopping the carriage so that it might be admired from every side, and Lady Wharncliffe, seeing the monument glowing in the evening light, considered it "a magnificent work of art."

Adelaide's admittedly chequered friendship with the Duchess of Kent was however sharply interrupted after the dreadful scene that occurred in 1836 during the King's birthday dinner at Windsor Castle. King William discovered that the Duchess had appropriated an extra suite of apartments in Kensington Palace without his leave and indeed in defiance of his express wishes. Rising to reply to the toast of his health, he was unable to contain his anger and found he could endure this "most unwarrantable liberty" no longer. He referred to the approach of Princess Victoria's coming-of-age and then scathingly burst out that, in the event of his death, he would "have the satisfaction of leaving the royal authority to the personal exercise of that Young Lady ... and not in the hands of a person, now near me, who is surrounded by evil advisers and who is herself incompetent to act with propriety..." The Queen was deeply distressed, the Princess burst into tears, and the Duchess of Kent, flushed with rage, ordered her carriage to be on hand as soon as possible.

Within a year, Victoria was Queen Regnant, and with the departure of the dowager Queen Adelaide to the retirement of Bushey and Marlborough House, the Lodge perhaps knew more solitude than at any time since Sarah Churchill's day. There was only the gardener, the housekeeper and the indoor gardener who tended the conservatory, the elements of a bucolic triangular comedy. Once again there was talk of pulling the place down to the ground now that it no longer served a useful purpose. In February 1840, however, when Royal Lodge was at its most damp and dismal, a new champion came on the scene in the person of the young Queen's new husband, the twenty-year-old Prince Albert.

II

Prince Albert may seem an unexpected presence at Royal Lodge, linking it in spirit with the Gothic dining-room of his own Rosenau; but he perhaps enjoyed his first Windsor picnic there and may have ridden to Virginia Water with the gentle, fair Queen Adelaide during his brief visit to England in 1836. When she came to the Throne, the young Queen Victoria equally liked nothing better than to circle Virginia Water, "a beautiful ride." Three years later the lake and the Lodge undoubtedly figured in that unforgettable day of courtship when Albert and his brother Ernest rode out with the young Queen, and Victoria first expressed her preference by riding between Lord Melbourne on his mettlesome white-faced horse and the handsome Albert "with whom I talked a good deal." Prince Albert's affection for the Lodge was manifest when, as a young husband of six months, "the husband, not the master of the house" he wrote to his father of the difficulties that besieged him even in planning and insisting on a new garden layout at Windsor Castle, and in the ensuing correspondence he jubilantly stressed twice within a month, that he had saved the Lodge from destruction.

"It took me much trouble to get this (the new pleasure-grounds) settled," he wrote on August 2nd 1840, "as it did before to save the existence of the fishing temple and George IV's cottage, which were to have been taken away. These are now safe." Two days later, the Office of Works approved estimates of £400 on a plan for "adapting the rooms adjoining the Conservatory" and Prince Albert was again able to report jubilantly, "I have saved the charming King's Cottage, with the greenhouse, which was to have been demolished as useless, by installing Anson there." George Anson, son of a Dean of Chester and formerly Lord Melbourne's private secretary, had been one of the first appointments to the Prince's personal staff and, although Albert was distrustful at first, the firm friendship of the two men ended only with Anson's sudden death nine years later.

"He was my only intimate friend," Albert was to say brokenly to the Queen. "We went through everything together... He was almost like a brother." But Anson's premature end lay in the unguessed future, like Albert's own, on the August afternoon when Victoria went to the cottage to inspect the new arrangements and opined in her journal that the house was very small but would do very well, "such a sweet spot and the garden is so nice." In reality, it was indeed far too small for a young married man, his wife and children, and the Ansons moved out within three years.

Then the plump little Queen again visited the old scene "so pretty and peaceful" and went "all over the house and into the garden, which was in great beauty, full of flowers." Now she herself was a wife and the mother of three children, and beginning to wonder whether it would not be well to have some small place of special retirement for just she and Albert to enjoy on their own. By the autumn the possibility was being discussed with Queen Victoria's Prime Minister, Sir Robert Peel. A cruise along the South Coast led to the discovery of the rival attractions of the Isle of Wight and in particular of Osborne, where the owner, Lady Isabella Blachford, was asking £30,000 as the purchase price, claiming that the estate was "ripe for building development."

Both Peel and Anson urged that Royal Lodge could be developed at an outlay of many thousands less. But as soon as

Victoria had rented Osborne for a trial holiday all the happy memories of the Lodge were cast to the winds and Osborne was victoriously purchased, ultimately — thanks to diplomatic bargaining on Peel's part — for £26,000. In 1846, when Victoria and Albert moved into their new re-built island mansion, the *Visitor's Windsor* could mention only that the "dining-room, conservatory and gardener's cottage" of the Royal Lodge were "preserved for occasional fetes."

The Queen in fact used it as her Aunt Adelaide had done before her, as a pleasant port of call for afternoon tea, driving there through the park in her pony chair, with servants following behind with the hampers. For ten years Royal Lodge thus remained in the pleasant side-wings of Royal Family life, making no demands on the Office of Works (or Woods and Forests) and with little expense to the taxpayer. Then, in the torrid June of 1856, the architects and surveyors were aroused from their torpor and required to fix a roof of painted deal over the old flat roof, to help insulate the hot little rooms "and keep the house cool in summer." The architect, Mr. Storey, was also required to provide an extra room, an effect he economically achieved merely by partitioning a ground-floor kitchen and moving the kitchen range.

The reason for these exertions was a pale, poetic, musical and painstaking boy who was to use the Lodge as a prison-house for his studies. Queen Victoria's second son, Alfred, Duke of Edinburgh, has managed to get himself excluded from British social history chiefly by his habit in later life of wearing too many rings on his fingers, but he is perpetuated in his mother's journals and letters as "dear 'Affie'," the "good, dear, clever, promising, child," the "good, dear, clever, odd boy." His dear face and "amiable, happy, merry temper" the Queen could not praise enough, while the heir to the throne, the wretched Bertie, with his "systematic idleness, laziness, disregard of everything" filled the royal mama's heart with indignation.

Affie was three years junior to the Prince of Wales, the future Edward VII, and the two boys were joint victims of the Prince Consort's shocking educational discipline. The rules were laid down that the two should be tired out physically at the end of every day by means of riding, drill and gymnastics, and under the regime of Frederick Gibbs, the tutor, this included "a regular course of military exercises under the instruction of a Sergeant." Perhaps dark, curling guilts of his own boyhood perpetuated the Prince Consort's insistence on fatigue: he must have foreseen words of doom in a report that Prince Alfred was "much too young and too yielding."

Prince Albert's solution in this moral dilemma was his decision that the two brothers should be rigidly separated and on June 3rd 1856, the eleven-year-old Prince Alfred was led away, sobbing bitterly. At Windsor, the Queen accepted that the parting of the brothers was for their own good, as Lady Longford has said, but the elder boy was found so "very low" in spirits that evening that he was accorded the unusual privilege of being allowed to sit with his mother during dinner while she tried to comfort him. We do not know whether Alfred cried himself to sleep, or stifled his sobs in fear of his new tutor, that first night at Royal Lodge. He had shown an infantile interest in the Royal Navy, "his love for the Blue Jackets," as his father termed it, and although he was settled at the Lodge with an Army officer of the Royal Engineers, Lieutenant John Cowell, his instructor was clearly under the Prince Consort's injunction to keep "the spontaneous wish of a young spirit" well in mind.

Prince Alfred might have made an excellent Ranger of Windsor Great Park; he had a bent for natural history and architecture and devoted "every free moment to his mechanical constructions," as his father noted. But the nearest that destiny ever brought Prince Alfred in this direction was that his name was given to one of the most famous of the prize-winning royal Windsor bulls. Yet Affie's prime asset was his remarkable perseverance, so unlike sullen Bertie. Some chance remark made him suppose that it would please his parents to have him join them in their musical duets and he learned to play the violin in secret at Royal Lodge. It was "an example of his perseverance … wishing to surprise us," the Prince Consort wrote to his own brother, the Duke Ernest, in Saxe-Coburg.

Ultimately, in manhood, Alfred took laurels and presumably applause when he played with an amateur orchestra in a charity concert at the Queen's Hall, the only member of the Royal Family ever to perform in a public concert hall. He was also, oddly, the only British royalty ever to be at the receiving end of an assassin's bullet, not forgetting Sipido's alarming near-miss when the Prince of Wales's railway train was leaving Brussels. Affie's adversary was an oddity, a Fenian in Australia, pledged to destroy British rule in Ireland, who got close enough to the Prince to put a bullet between his ninth and tenth ribs. The patient recovered in the care of two nurses newly trained by Florence Nightingale and, having diced with death, he found himself in a ready frame of mind to marry the Czar of Russia's somewhat formidable only daughter, the twenty-year-old Grand Duchess Marie. Queen Victoria rewarded his docility by creating him Duke of Edinburgh and the marriage was celebrated amid scenes of fantastic splendour in the Winter Palace. The Duchess filled Clarence House in London with her ikons and bore her husband a son and four daughters, one of whom became the glamorous, amorous, publicity-loving Queen Marie of Romania.

Marie complained that in girlhood she seldom saw her father. His naval career was successful, well-praised and obscure. He was more often in Malta, where rumour accorded him a full-fledged illicit domestic establishment, than in London. In 1893 he succeeded as Duke of Saxe-Coburg and Gotha, and so further removed himself from the scenes of British history, and he died in his dutiful German exile just six months before his mother at Osborne. But now we are treading far into the future, far ahead of the young Prince, studying, drilling, flexing his muscles under watchful eyes, fiddling in secret at Royal Lodge.

III

Through these mid-Victorian years George IV's cast-iron conservatory gradually rusted away, increasingly unloved, less-tended and shabby. A succession of short-term summer guests sat amid the plants in wicker chairs, and an ecstatic American visitor of the 1850s thought that the Lodge, nestling in its garden of roses and fuchsias, was one of the most captivating cottages he had ever seen. But in this quiescent decade the focus of life shifted to an even smaller cottage down the drive occupied by a foreman in charge of park improvements, the so-called Keeper of the King's Ride, who drove round in a donkey-cart to inspect the continuous lopping and tidying undertaken by drafts of soldiers returned from the Crimea.

The keeper's cottage is still there, with its own hedged garden, a unique hideaway for perhaps some future young royal couple who may thus enjoy total privacy within the chestnut-fenced domain of Royal Lodge itself. The last of the older neighbouring buildings, the tiny chapel which George IV had built for Lady Conyngham, was demolished in 1862 during the "Windsor fever" — as *The Builder* termed it — of establishing memorials to the Prince Consort. The foundation stone of a new chapel, grandiloquently at first called All Saints' Church, was laid in November 1863, by Queen Victoria's eldest daughter, the Crown Princess of Prussia. The building was consecrated a year later, but the final £3,400 required for completion somehow sank into the quicksands of diminishing grief and financial mismanagement.

It is fortunate that the plans of the architect, Arthur W. Blomfield, were never fully carried out, for the church would otherwise have been as large again, with a detached campanile, and proliferating chapels and vestries. Happily, the vines cloaking its pale brick and stone, the chapel appears smaller than it is, though six hundred can in fact be seated in the stained-deal pews. In the interior, a century of family memorials has masked the brick walls, and although the columns and small shafts in the nave are carved of stone, the present Queen nevertheless worships in one of the plainest religious edifices in England.

In 1865, when the Prince of Wales realised that his newly-acquired residence of Sandringham Hall was too small and damp and would have to be rebuilt, Queen Victoria suggested that he should adapt Royal Lodge instead, as a country retreat nearer than Sandringham, and the Queen even went so far as to hint that it would be more convenient for Ascot week. Her overtures were repulsed, for the Prince had set his heart on building a superb new mansion, and in Norfolk he was always at least a telegraph-length from his Mama's reproaches. Meanwhile, when the fortunes of the Lodge seemed at their lowest ebb, Queen Victoria's third daughter, Affie's favourite sister, Princess Helena (Lenchen), married the penniless Prince Christian of Schleswig-Holstein and so set a fresh cycle of events in train. Seven years later, when they had four children, the demands of their growing family compelled a move from Frogmore to Cumberland Lodge. The comptroller of their improvident household, Colonel George Grant Gordon, then settled into Royal Lodge and so the fortunes of the two buildings, evoking the ghosts of the old upper and lower lodges, were to be reunited for another score of years.

A fire had diminished the early Georgian glories of Cumberland Lodge, though not the extraordinary extent of the stables, and the family lived at first in a constant welter of crises with their new ground landlords of the department of Woods and Forests. "They are slower and pay more for their workmen and are more disagreeable than any people in the world," wrote Queen Victoria, at her most astringent, "Mr. Menzies is no architect... Mr. Menzies made a *bad job* in some ways of Cumberland Lodge and of the Woods and Forests in general." Mr. Menzies was presumably among those responsible for the inept Victorian domestic additions at Royal Lodge and the styling suggests that he also took on his shoulders the vandalism of pulling down George IV's conservatory and replacing it with a white painted, severely utilitarian structure of wood and glass resembling a greenhouse.

If Mr. Menzies in turn considered his royal clients unruly and demanding, this was nothing to the difficulties of the unfortunate chaplain of the Royal Lodge church when he filled his stained-deal pews with his Park congregation of six hundred, socially topped by the royals. "By all means," replied the Duke of Cambridge loudly, when the parson urged, "Let us pray!" When prayers for rain were offered the Almighty, the same Duke — he was Queen Mary's uncle — growled noisily, "Oh, God, how can you expect rain, my dear man, with the wind in the east?" In the nineteen-fifties, the last surviving baby of Cumberland Lodge, Princess Marie Louise, still remembered these unruly interruptions, if not the confusion of the chaplain when Princess Helena read a special prayer of intercession in a dock strike, and objected with annoyance, "That won't settle any strike!"

Colonel Gordon nominally lived at Royal Lodge for twenty-three years, a longer occupation than that of George IV and longer than any tenancy except that of the late Queen Mother. Off the main route of the social round of house-parties, the younger generation found it a small and accommodating house for inconspicuous entertainment, and clues hidden in the Windsor furniture inventories suggest that, at the gate of the "naughty nineties," the most interesting young bachelor in all England had a snug little apartment there for a time. This was Prince Albert Victor, Duke of Clarence and Avondale, the eldest son of the Prince of Wales (later Edward VII) and thus heir-presumptive to the throne.

Like his Uncle Affie, Prince Albert Victor — Prince Eddy as he was known in the Family — has been pushed into the shadows of royal history and yet his tragic youthful death from pneumonia changed the dynasty. Had he lived, he would have succeeded his father, Edward VII, as King in 1910, and George V might never have reigned.

Early in 1890 Colonel Gordon had the most politic reasons for making Prince Eddy comfortable at the Lodge. Up at Cumberland Lodge Princess Helena had two marriageable daughters and it seemed that the volatile and readily susceptible Eddy might have his emotions skilfully steered in their direction, given local opportunity and time. When he was twenty-six years old, the bachelor Prince returned from a tour of India looking, as Queen Victoria said, "dreadfully thin … and pale and drawn" and it would appear that Colonel Gordon struck while the moment was opportune with his offer of a restful retreat. The apartment Prince Eddy occupied at Royal Lodge cannot now be identified but, the superstitious may take note, it was listed in the Windsor records of the day as Room 13.

Prince Eddy was adoped by his sisters for his gaiety, his kindness and consideration, his smartness and insistence on good grooming; and he found that his apartment at Royal Lodge lacked only one amenity, a good mirror. Precisely this, "a good mirror", was therefore solicited from the Windsor stores, and by this Eddy no doubt meant a clear large looking glass which would adequately reflect his gentle fawn-like eyes and waxed moustache, his "collars and cuffs," but the Lord Chamberlain's store-keeper took him at his word and provided an eighteenth-century Chinese Chippendale mirror "of upright rectangular form, contained in a border, also of looking-glass, of broken scroll outline, most elaborately framed in pinewood, gilt." We need not dwell on what this treasure may have reflected in Prince Eddy's room. After his death it was returned to Windsor Castle and placed deep in the lower stores, until unexpectedly revived for an Edwardian awakening when it was hung in the King's closet.

Princess Helena's indirect hospitality might have been devised with more caution had she realised her young nephew's reputation with women. At Cambridge, and then during his army life in Dublin, his seductive attractions alarmed even his broad-minded father and acrid words on Prince Eddy's "dissipated life" flowed from Queen Victoria's private pen. At a higher level than the bedroom, the impressionable

Eddy rapidly fell in and out of love with a string of eligible princesses with a facility equally dismaying to his elders. He proposed to his cousin, Princess Alix of Hesse, who had to reply by letter in May 1890, that much as it pained her to pain him and much as she liked him as a cousin she knew they would not be happy together. In that same month, he professed to fall wildly in love with Princess Helene of Orleans, a match which because of her Catholic religion seemed to Queen Victoria "utterly impossible." The beguiling Eddy nevertheless saw that his affections for his tall brunette charmer were returned with unmistakable Gallic clarity and this response prepared him to rush across country with Helene and plead at Balmoral for the Queen's help rather than her refusal.

Sentimentally touched, his grandmother unexpectedly agreed to do all she could for the young lovers. Up at Cumberland Lodge the youngest princess, Marie Louise, evidently accepted the hint that her own prospects of marrying Eddy and becoming Queen of England were tenuous; and she felt flattered by the direct attentions of her "beau ideal of a cavalry officer," Prince Aribert of Anhalt. Her engagement to this romantic stranger was announced at the end of the year. Alas, the marriage was to end in divorce and it may be of emotional significance that at the end of her life, Princess Marie Louise did not mention the Duke of Clarence in her memoirs.

In any event, the Helene affair was officially at an end even before Marie Louise's wedding. Princess Helene's father would not permit a marriage involving a change of religion and the Pope confirmed this verdict. Hope must have flared anew for the elder unmarried daughter still at Cumberland Lodge. But by late summer Prince Eddy was undecided in his admiration for the beautiful debutante Lady Sybil St. Clair Erskine and his certainly eligible cousin at Richmond, Princess May of Teck. "I wonder if you really love me a little?" he wrote to Lady Sybil. In December the vacillations were resolved and soon the crowds were cheering the radiant Princess May (the future Queen Mary).

None of these scenes were necessarily attached to Royal Lodge, for Prince Eddy was often with his regiment in York. But the disappointed mama of Cumberland Lodge sallied forth and could not resist being "positively rude" to Princess May and her mother, as Queen Victoria unfailingly recorded, though the "little inexplicable moment" at Marlborough House was quickly over and quickly forgotten. Instead of coping with a new bridegroom and a national romance, Princess Helena of Schleswig-Holstein had to solace a husband who had received a bullet in his eye in a shooting accident in Windsor Park. Meanwhile, in the first days of the New Year of 1892, Prince Eddy looked into his opulent mirror at Royal Lodge for the last time. He went to London to attend a funeral where he caught a chill that resolved into pneumonia, and on January 14th the shock of his sudden death at Sandringham seemed to the majority of people the most sensational news event the nation had ever known.

IV

Princess May married George, Duke of York, the younger brother. And at a ball at the Fishing Temple at Virginia Water, late on a June evening in 1894, the Prince of Wales stopped the orchestra to make an announcement. "It is with pleasure that I am able to inform you of the birth of a son to the Duke and Duchess of York," he told the throng in his gruff tones. "I propose a toast to the young Prince." This is the first we hear of the Duke of Windsor, and almost the last of the Fishing Temple in foremost affairs.

The old Queen died at Osborne and Edward VII succeeded to the Throne. The Edwardian years at Royal Lodge were a serene and unhurried phase when old Lord Bridport, who had been born only nine years after the Battle of Trafalgar, sat puffing his cigar in the garden on summer days, and thought perhaps of his surprise in boyhood on learning he was a grand-nephew of none other than Lord Nelson. Nevertheless, he elected for the Army, he served his pensioned years as a groom-in-waiting and he came to Royal Lodge in 1896 when widowed and already aged eighty. He lived indeed into his ninetieth year. In 1904 his successor in the grace-and-favour tenancy was the King's close friend, Sir Arthur Ellis, ex-Sandhurst and Grenadier Guards, formerly an equerry to the King as Prince of Wales and now comfortably settled in the new Court hierarchy as comptroller to the Lord Chamberlain. With his insatiable interest in the curiosities of ceremonial, this post at St. James's ideally suited him. In one mood he would excitedly denounce the lower classes as "rabid rebels," and in more mellow vein he was the man who devised the glittering evening Courts that cast such a benign glaze of Imperial affluence over the uppermost Edwardian social strata.

He and the King stage-managed the pageantry of the courts together, agreeing on details to the last breeches-button. The King's assistant secretary, Frederick Ponsonby, said of Ellis that he had visited every Court in Europe with King Edward and "had an unrivalled knowledge of the way things were done." An affable raconteur, he revelled in discovering and conveying to his cronies the hot gossip that no Russians were entitled to wear the Russian Cross of St. George, not even the Czar, because its qualification was to have commanded a victorious army in the field, and that at one time the Duke of Wellington was one of only three members of the Order in the world. He discovered with joy that members of the Austrian Order of the Golden Fleece took a sacred oath always to wear the badge of the Order, and so had special collars made for the badge which they wore at night in bed. With his own zest for decorations, the King adored such tales, and dinners were followed by choice cigars and excellent brandy at Royal Lodge when King and courtier yarned far into the night.

It was Ellis one day who sent a complete Garter riband to Benjamin Constant, the artist, in order that a royal portrait could be accurate in colour. The artist mistakenly jumped to the conclusion that the Garter had been conferred upon him, and on discovering the truth was so put out that he refused to correct his canvas. No doubt Sir Arthur Ellis lived in a dream world. In his day twelve servants were kept at the Lodge in addition to three outdoor gardeners: the service was impeccable whenever the King and Queen Alexandra came to lunch. From old letters one glimpses the sparkle of silver and crystal, the urbane conversation, the footmen circulating, the smell of perfume and food. One catches the easy laughter, and the complacent glances at signed royal photographs massed in the background amid the bijouterie and the flowers. The Wyatville dining-room, evidently unpartitioned in those days, basked as the scene of these occasions; and the dishes were conveyed by a nearby service-lift from the basement kitchen to the "old hall," as the dining-room was then known.

One cannot tell where Sir Arthur and Lady Ellis slept all their servants. Between the years 1904 and 1907 the courtly owner was apparently responsible for building an extra storey and so gave his guests four additional bedrooms and a bathroom, besides the four bedrooms and two bathrooms already in use. With two sons and five daughters his family requirements were not inconsiderable. The nearby cottage outside provided two rooms and a bathroom for bachelors and the guests strolled to bed through an avenue of geraniums and flowering hydrangeas. The three gardeners were concerned only with tending the lawns and flowering shrubs and providing floral decorations for the house, for there was no kitchen garden. In winter, one year, they were occupied in planting a new yew hedge which took in more ground. And all the splendour magnificently ended in character. At a gala performance at Covent Garden Sir Arthur Ellis was so overcome by the presence of eleven royalties and their entourages, the fabulous glitter of Orders and decorations and dresses, that he suffered a fatal heart attack and died on the plush-seated chair, his satin programme still on his knees.

His widow survived him for ten years. Then, in 1919, the Dugdales arrived. The names of Colonel Frank and Lady Eva Dugdale perhaps strike the eye listlessly now in the old lists of members of the Royal Household, but when Eva Dugdale died in 1940, Queen Mary reflected, "I had known her for fifty-five years!" She was a Greville, only daughter of the fourth Earl of Warwick, and Queen Mary first met her when, as the eighteen-year-old Princess May, she expectantly returned from Florence to the pleasures of London life. Eva — Little Eva as she was at first called from her diminutive stature and, later, Little Bird, from her birdlike look and fluttering ways, was seven years older and she became the natural confidante of May's first engagement to Prince Eddy and her second betrothal to Prince George, the Duke of York. She then became the new Duchess of York's lady-in-waiting, and for a quarter-century, when the shy and retiring May became Princess of Wales and then Queen, Eva Dugdale was Queen Mary's right hand.

Her own marriage in no way impaired the relationship. A post in the Household was found for her Yorkshire husband

and, at Edward VII's Coronation, when the new Princess of Wales "processed" through Westminster Abbey, it was Eva who supported one corner of her heavy purple and ermine train while Lady Mary Lygon carried the other. Nine years passed, and when Queen Mary went to Buckingham Palace to rearrange her furnishings in the private apartments, the Dugdales worked with her, helping to hang pictures, arrange china, shift furniture until the task was finished and Queen Mary could write triumphantly, "Eva dined with me in my green room which looks charming." After the First World War, Lady Dugdale suffered a stroke and, on her recovery, was assigned the Royal Lodge, which had stood empty for two years. It was then the Queen's turn to help rearrange her friend's treasures in the rooms, the souvenirs brought back from the Delhi Durbar, the gifts from the old Duchess of Mecklenburg-Strelitz, all her accumulation of royal keepsakes.

One other stray circumstance must be recorded. In the old days it had been a punctilious tradition that Lady Eve should be present with the Duke and Duchess of York at meals which, as the Duke of Windsor once said, meant that he and his brother were hardly ever alone with their parents. Although she relinquished Royal Lodge in 1925, the Little Bird lived to see the outcome, in the Abdication, of those early fledgling habits.

From the year 1926 onwards, the Fetherstonhaughs enjoyed the last twilight of the old days. The huge stables nearby at Cumberland Lodge were an advantage in the intricate business of race-training and breeding, and a private telephone line was first linked to Royal Lodge from Windsor Castle. When Mrs. Fetherstonhaugh rode in the sixth carriage in the Ascot procession down the course, no one realised that she was the lady who executed George V's betting orders and kept his bookmaking account. When the King won, his hoarse hearty voice would chaff her on the private line. He used to buy stamps with his profits, and was always pleased that the occasional gains of that one hobby could supposedly subsidise another interest.

And so we have come through nearly three centuries since Captain John Byfield moved into his "small, decayed tenement" in lieu of a pay packet, and King Charles strode for exercise across Windsor Park. We have seen Sarah, Duchess of Marlborough, matching up materials and conning over her accounts; we have watched the Duke of Cumberland with his horses and the Sandbys with their sketchbooks, John Nash with his estimates and the Prince Regent with his tepid card-parties … all the personages and events of passing time like autumnal oak leaves blowing across the Royal Lodge drive.

10: THE KING'S HOME

I

The year 1936 opened with none knowing that it was to be unique in nearly five centuries of British history as the year of the three Kings. The Duke and Duchess of York were alone together that New Year at Royal Lodge. The Duchess was in bed, recovering from an attack of pneumonia that had left her weak and shaken, and they had never known the house so silent or so strangely empty. They had indeed never been so isolated. The children and their nursemaids had gone to Sandringham for Christmas, and the hush that settled around the house was in keeping with the weather, mild with occasional rain beating against the windows, like an insistent, reiterated theme of lull and impending storm.

The Duke may have found leisure to glance at his collation of Royal Lodge history. All the notes and quotations that Owen Morshead had sent him from Windsor now seemed so nearly complete. Then, in the second week of the year, gales whipped the deadwood from the trees, alternate sleet and snow masked the garden and in mid-January Queen Mary sent a message saying that the King was ill and that she wished the Duke to come to Sandringham to help her with the house-party. The Duke of York left Royal Lodge in response to his mother's appeal, and returned home to his wife three days later, distressed that his father's illness had taken a much graver turn. He had hardly entered the house than a fresh urgent summons came for him to return to Sandringham. Alone and anxious with her lady-in-waiting, Lady Helen Graham, the Duchess of York listened to the solemn radio bulletins on the night of January 20th–21st telling that the King's life was drawing peacefully to its close.

Shortly after midnight, the telephone rang and her husband at Sandringham told her the final news. The Duchess's sad, resigned emotion was reflected in a letter to her doctor, Lord Dawson of Penn, which I venture briefly to quote, "…when you came to see me at Royal Lodge, we spoke of the King, and how vital he was to us in this country … it is wonderful to know that his rest came so quietly. He was getting so tired…" But when her husband returned from Sandringham, it was as more than Duke of York, for he was heir-presumptive to the Throne. Outwardly, as the Duchess said, life went on the same, but everything was different now.

The difference was that when the Duke and his wife went over to visit his brother at Fort Belvedere, it was the King they saw, the new King Edward VIII, and when the piper marched around the table, it was the King's piper, playing "Over the sea to Skye." We need not reiterate the overfamiliar drama of Abdication Year too fully in these pages. Mrs. Simpson, the pivot of that story, visited Royal Lodge only once, coming over for tea one weekend with the King, and Marion Crawford long afterwards remembered her "distinctly proprietary way of speaking to the new King… She drew him to the window and suggested how certain trees might be moved, and a part of a hill taken away to improve the view."

The strain of a tactless remark could be felt in the room. An American might not have realised that her host and hostess were tenants, and tenants at that by grace-and-favour of the King. The ten-year-old Princess Elizabeth gazed at the visitor and, after her mother suggested that the children should be taken for a walk in the woods, the Princess asked her governess, uneasily, "Who is she?" Months later, the public drama of the last days of the reign of Edward VIII centred upon Fort Belvedere while the more homely rooms of Royal Lodge witnessed the family uncertainty and disbelief, the whirlwind of personal emotions that tightened at last to grief and dismay of King Edward's irrevocable resolve to relinquish the Throne.

On Saturday, December 5th, the Duke of York, arriving at Royal Lodge for the weekend as usual, had perhaps expected a message and found there was none and telephoned his elder brother for news. "Come and see me on Sunday," the King replied. "I'll tell you my decision when I've made up my mind." For two days the agony centred on the telephone. The Duke rang again on Sunday and was told that the King was in conference and would call him back, but the promised telephone call never came. On Monday the Duke called once more and the King could only say that he might see him that evening. Through the day the man who would so soon be summoned to the Throne himself endured, as best he could, as he said, the "awful and ghastly suspense of waiting." On the Monday evening the King telephoned to suggest a meeting after dinner. "No," said the Duke, "I will come at once."

He went to the Fort to face at last the dreadful truth of the decision, and returned to Royal Lodge to break the crucial news to his wife and have dinner with her. Then, he hurried back to the Fort later that evening to be with his brother. "I had to be there," he explained, "to try and help him in his hour of need." Now all was over, save the partings. In London, on Tuesday, the Duchess of York fell ill with influenza and the doctors sent her to bed. On the Wednesday, when Fort Belvedere was still under siege by the newspaper world, it was arranged that Queen Mary should meet the still reigning King at the Lodge. On its north-east slope of the hill, the rose-pink house was cloaked in mist when the Queen arrived with her daughter, the Princess Royal, after lunch, and presently mother and son were left alone together in the drawing-room.

"She was already waiting when I arrived," the Duke of Windsor later described the meeting in his memoirs. "She still disapproved and was bewildered by my action, but now that it was all over, her heart went out to her hard-pressed son." Through the French windows he could see the fog thickening in the garden as he gave an account of all the six days of incessant discussion with the Prime Minister and others, and of Mrs. Simpson's departure from England. Queen Mary murmured, with an unexpected impulse of tenderness, "And to me the worst thing is that you won't be able to see her for so long."

The next day Royal Lodge took on the pilot in the person of Lord Wigram who had served the inner mechanics of monarchy for a quarter of a century as Assistant Private Secretary and then Private Secretary to King George V. In the early transitional stage of the new reign he had served Edward VIII and none knew better the business of statecraft. His role was more important than its title implies, for the Private Secretary is the official channel of communication between the Sovereign and their Government. Now he came to the Lodge, still with the look of the cavalry officer, to prepare the Duke of York for his imminent passage into kingship. He was present, too, at what the Duke of York called "a terrible lawyer interview" which ended smoothly with the disposition of family property, of Sandringham and so forth, effected harmoniously. That evening the Duke of York dined with Wigram and Sir Edward Peacock (who managed the affairs of the Duchy of Cornwall) before he returned to London and faced the unexpected, cheering crowds.

When dinner was served at Royal Lodge the following evening, George VI was King. His wife, his Queen, was still in bed with flu at No. 145, but the abdicated monarch had expressed the wish to have dinner at the Lodge, a farewell family dinner party. The other guests were his two younger brothers, his mother, his sister and his aunt and uncle, the Athlones. "Dinner passed pleasantly enough under the circumstances," the Duke of Windsor noted afterwards. But he had left Fort Belvedere for the last time and nothing more awaited him in England except his final broadcast from Windsor Castle. The house was shrouded in fog when the steward announced that Mr. Walter Monckton had arrived to take His Royal Highness to the Castle. And then, in Queen Mary's poignant words in her journal, "came the dreadful goodbye."

II

Before he came to the Throne, the then Duke of York had benefited financially under the will and family settlements of his father, and many long-cherished plans for Royal Lodge had been carried into effect during 1936, foremost among them the sunken garden created for his wife below the southern terrace near their bedroom windows. When Mr. Russell Page was consulted, his client already had a list of plants of sentimental significance that might be included. It was to be akin, if possible, to a garden his wife had known in her earlier youth at Glamis and yet, since counterparts are never possible, it was first and foremost to suit the Lodge itself. It should provide roses of every form and be neighboured by an old-fashioned mixed border with lupins, irises, pyrethrums, peonies, mignonette and lavender. The professional gardener is faced so often with demands for fragrance and colour and abundance

172

but the owner of Royal Lodge knew what he wanted, having expended thought and care, and his wishes were to be brilliantly realised.

Mr. G. A. Jellicoe, a landscape architect of the highest ability, was also called in to design a new improved west terrace and to link and unify the new garden features. To avoid a skimped effect the terrace was to be as wide as the Wyatville saloon or drawing-room from which it opened. It is, in fact, some eighteen feet wide, flagged with non-slip artificial paving, within broad crenellated walls that echo the silhouette of the house. Shallow stairways lead down to the lawn past stone-walled beds, filled in spring with tulips and later in bedding plants, and so house and garden have no firm demarcation. There may at first have seemed too stony an effect. If so, it was quickly softened by the introduction of pyramid box trees in elegant tubs along the terrace walls, a dozen or more like green sentinels, and these in turn soon had their smaller counterparts in tubs against the house.

To provide counterpoint and shelter at the north end of the terrace, a white-painted trellis was designed against the hedge, topped by amusing plinths for which rampant gilt lions, based on the heraldic beasts at Hampton Court, were carved in wood by the sculptor, Alan King. This formed a pleasant nook for dinner out of doors on a summer evening. With these and other alterations, a troublesome old rock garden, which the Yorks had never cared about, was gradually erased. It is characteristic that, on becoming King George VI, the owner of Royal Lodge suggested that visitors should keep quiet about this change. There were thousands of people who enjoyed rock gardening, he realised, whom he did not wish to deter by the royal example.

The new King's need for secretarial and business space at the Lodge, as well as the Queen's inexhaustible hospitality, also prompted a considerable extension embodied in the three-storied wing which faced the forecourt. This enlargement was achieved without the slightest intrusion into the home-like atmosphere of the royal couple's own original apartments. The King's office lay to the right, close to the front door, and the secretarial rooms extended beyond it towards the domestic regions. The upper rooms comprised guest suites, each with bathrooms. The soft pink colourwash diminished the otherwise excessive effect of the sweeping line of fifteen windows that overlooked the forecourt, and pleasantly unified the exterior. The string-courses, the flat roof and the windows, matched those of the two-storey wings on either side, and at one time the rooftop was decked with finials to match the decorations above the saloon, but these were found fussy and were removed.

Could George IV have bowled up in his phaeton he would have seen that his successor had retained the atmosphere of his own Royal Lodge, the same enclosed forecourt, the same wings of shrubbery, the same masking of impressive size, achieved in the contemporary spirit of another age. The gaiety of the Regency found an expressive echo in the pink walls, the lavender-grey woodwork, and the striped sunblinds that presently decked Wyatville's saloon windows. As has been mentioned, King George VI had Melville's 1830 lithograph of "The King's Cottage" hung in his bedroom. Identification of the trees in the print was difficult but it pleased the new King to think that George IV's two cedars of Lebanon were still in existence, now ninety feet high and fifty feet in span of branch; and perhaps George IV sometimes took tea, as George VI and his Queen now liked to do, beneath the ancient oak of seven yards girth that still shadowed the lawn near the octagon room.

King George VI suggested at one time that it would be pleasant to link the two kings of Royal Lodge in joint commemoration, and the King commissioned Herbert Palliser, the sculptor, to prepare a plaque in which the numerals IV and VI should be interwoven. Evidently intended to be affixed to the corner exterior of the octagon room, the plaque was completed but never secured in position. During the war it was placed for safekeeping in the Windsor stores and now cannot be found.

Sir John Wheeler Bennett has affirmed that the King wore himself out with his care for detail. No new addition could be made to a cottage, "no new tenant taken on, no employee discharged, no tree cut down, without the King's approval" but, in fact not every minor detail could be covered. The King directed that God's acre, the garden of the Royal Chapel, should be beautified and roses soon climbed the iron fences, and a wonderful wistaria was trained to the very belfry. (The gardener who tended the plot was also appointed the verger.) A clock was placed between the western windows so that the King might always know the time as he walked from his front door towards the chapel. Yet his attention to the garden was necessarily limited to the few minutes after morning service. Sometimes this was no more than a comprehensive glance that all was well. The King was compelled to spend hours in confidential sessions in his workroom, but he disliked to be shut away and preferred whenever possible to work while the life of the family went on around him. One of the few changes to denote that a King now toiled at the Lodge were in the two desks placed near the windows in the saloon. While the King worked at one, the Queen would quietly transact her own business at the other. During the war a rough wooden table, apparently of standard War Office issue, supported the extra burden of his dispatch boxes, and its very presence seemed to make the house a battle headquarters.

The architects who assisted the King at Royal Lodge minimise their services with professional reticence but they included Mr. Hubert Leadbetter, Mr. L. E. C. Osborne, the Crown Surveyor, Mr. Raymond Erith and, later on, the father-and-son partnership of Sydney and Rodney Tatchell. The Queen admired Mr. Raymond Erith's sensitive and skilful adaptations and additions to eighteenth-century work comparatively early in his practice, and later he was awarded the plum contract for the renovation of No. 10 Downing Street. The Tatchells' flair for the modern elements of Regency and for landscaping similarly commended itself and they were later responsible for the village of estate homes within Windsor Great Park and, in the present reign of Elizabeth II, the flats for Crown pensioners nearer Windsor town.

III

King George VI and his Queen spent the weekend before their Coronation in the peace of Royal Lodge in a mood of dedication and spiritual preparation. Through the week they lived now at Buckingham Palace instead of 145 Piccadilly but, as ever, the weekend return to the Lodge was a coming home. From April through till July each year, while the rhododendrons and azaleas flowered in succession, they tried to make their sojourn longer whenever public events permitted. Buckingham Palace provided no sense of escape but the garden of Royal Lodge offered nearly every afternoon the King's relaxation and respite. Then, after tea, the dispatch riders began to whirr down the drive, the Parliamentary boxes awaited him and he retired to his workroom. The hour unfortunately coincided with his daughters' reprieve from lessons. Their old rocking horses were placed in the hall near the study door; Princess Margaret liked to essay a ride with her elder sister to keep her company and the King could hear the rhythmic pounding of the rocking-horses as he worked.

Secluded and out of sight, down an embankment below the gardens of the Princesses' Little House, a swimming pool was also built, with changing rooms in a small white pavilion, but this was a luxury largely for the Princesses or for guests, like the tennis-court nearby in the woods after the King gave up play. In the autumn, the King liked to work in the woodland — there was always urgent replanting — and a trail of bonfire smoke was sometimes a sign that His Majesty was tidying up. Occasionally an air of conspiracy developed, especially when a birthday surprise was in preparation for the Queen. One may assume that a group of statuary in one of the long vistas thus appeared as if by magic one August day; a replica of the Charity group at St. Paul's, Walden Bury, the birthday girl's childhood home. Queen Mary often found an excuse to inspect the latest garden or woodland enterprise; and from her wish to understand her son's enjoyment there sprang her wartime "wooding" expeditions at Badminton when she attacked ivy, bramble and thinnings with unquenchable zest.

The outbreak of war found the King and Queen in London, but their daughters were sent for greater safety to Birkhall. Then, in the apparently inactive phase of the "phoney war," when the adversaries prepared for the future conflict, even Sandringham seemed relatively free from hostilities and, early in January 1940, the children's governess received a telegram from the Queen, "Please come to Royal Lodge. Can you come on the fifth?"

After that, the Royal Family were reunited. The Princesses were known by the public to be at "a house in the country," the identity of which was disclosed after the war as Windsor Castle, but the Princesses in fact remained at Royal Lodge until the 12th of May when it was known that the Germans were victorious in Norway and it was deemed prudent to shelter the Princesses within the armed security of the Castle itself.

A member of the Household has said that the Queen always "seemed to drop her cares at the gates of Royal Lodge," but its immunity was less than other country houses in Britain. The King and his equerries practised with rifles, pistols and tommy-guns at a shooting range in the garden. Regular stirrup-pump practice in readiness for incendiary bombs became a regular family routine near the swimming pool on Saturday afternoons. The old basement kitchen, though hardly impregnable, was strengthened with steel and mesh as a bomb shelter, and the whole house assumed a coat of greyish paint that made it less a landmark from the air. The Coats Mission was rehearsed for the withdrawal and safe escort of the Royal Family in the case of invasion. Near every bed in Royal Lodge in those days there stood a small suitcase ready packed in the name of "emergency clothes." During the night of September 9th 1940, when the first bombs fell on Buckingham Palace, the King and Queen were sleeping at Royal Lodge. Henceforth, like many Londoners with a chance of country accommodation, they slept at the Lodge each night and went up to the glass-littered metropolis every morning. Two months later, enemy planes were seen streaming over Windsor Great Park in full moonlight, and it seemed strange that no bombs were dropped … until the King heard that the attack was on Coventry. (He hurried there to give what psychological help he could the following day.)

More than eighty children were evacuated from London and other centres and billeted in houses in the Windsor Park, including Cumberland Lodge. It seemed dangerous to house them in so obvious a military objective as the Royal Lodge itself, a viewpoint tragically borne out shortly after the German Air Force began its "Baedeker bombing" against undefended Cathedral cities and historic centres such as Bath in retaliation for the Allied bombing of industrial centres. On either side of the entrance gate at the foot of the Royal Lodge drive there stood two groups of semi-detached brick cottages, humble and old-fashioned in appearance with their slate roofs and sashed windows. They housed gatekeepers and gardeners and had sheltered evacuee children earlier in the war. One day the King and Queen had news that made them hurry home from London as soon as possible. A bomb had destroyed the northern cottages and the gatekeeper and his wife had been killed. The war was thus tragically brought to their Majesties' own private domain.

Next came the V1s, the buzz-bombs, like pilotless planes, which trundled over England in the summer of 1944, and again Windsor was not exempt. They came at all hours, by day and night, some falling harmlessly on open land in the park or on Windsor racecourse. The two Princesses were thus literally under fire on one occasion when a bomb came over as they sat with a Girl Guides party cooking sausages around a camp fire. The children lay down, the Guide captain flung herself across the future Queen, the bomb passed over and cut out a few seconds later and fell near enough for the children to be shaken by the explosion. Altogether two hundred high-explosive bombs fell within the King's estate, though mercifully with little corresponding loss of life.

It has been said that the war killed George VI, and before his first operation in 1949 five doctors testified that the strain of kingship in those arduous years had "appreciably affected his resistance to physical fatigue." The King and Queen returned to Royal Lodge from the wild enthusiasm of the victory celebrations "rather jaded from it all," as the King wrote, and like everyone else they turned eagerly to the tasks of reconstruction and the happiness of resuming normal family life.

About a mile west of Royal Lodge, a new "village" adjacent to the Crown Estate workshops was the King's contribution to the post-war problem of rehousing. Twenty-eight new houses were grouped around a triangular green under the plan of the architects, Sydney and Rodney Tatchell, and the King and Queen often came over from the Lodge to inspect the work in different stages. It embodies in many ways George VI's own ideas on town-planning: the hamlet complete to its own village hall and grocery store, and the latter probably the only shop in the country bearing a medallion of Garter blue with a royal cypher above its doorway. Meanwhile, the blitzed entrance cottages were also rebuilt under the care of the same architects, and the opportunity was taken to enlarge each pair, north and south, into a terrace of three, coated with stucco in the Regency style, with entrance doors embellished by columns and pediments of the most graceful character. Later the cottages were linked to the two gate lodges by long ornamental balustrades, forming an entrance that today blends an airy charm with formal elegance.

One suspects that the architects deferred to the present Queen Mother's feminine preferences, and certainly much of the work and planning was undertaken at the time of her husband's illness. But the Queen's harmonious understanding of her husband's wishes constituted but a fraction of their married felicity. In 1948, when they celebrated their Silver Wedding, one of her gifts to him was a crystal casket fashioned in the form of a temple, with its transparent sides engraved by Laurence Whistler with the symbols of her husband's interests: gardening tools, books, sporting trophies and the instruments of architecture and design. On the lid was inscribed a poem, *From the Queen to the King:* "Fond hope: to compass on a page so brief… The testament of Love! — on timid glass…" Near the base of the temple a polished door opens at a touch and, as it does so, light floods through the crystal walls, bringing the scrolled garlands and the depiction of Cupid's altar into shining relief. In many ways, the illumined casket reflects the testament of Royal Lodge itself.

Soon the house glowed rose-pink again and family life flooded in. One wartime Christmas Eve, Prince Philip had come to dinner, and as Princess Margaret wrote to a friend, they had put out all the lights afterwards and listened to ghost stories. The firelight was congenial to Prince Philip and Princess Elizabeth. The Lodge quietly witnessed much of the happiness of their courtship, and now they came over as a young married couple from Windlesham Moor, visiting their parents. Sunday lunch at the Lodge assumed a new significance and the house seemed to don a fresh aura of youthful welcome. There were afternoon walks to see the restoration of the Savill Gardens, where beds and paths solid with weeds were scythed after the wartime years of enforced neglect. Windsor Park's contribution to the food problem had seen the intensive cultivation of two thousand acres and, being incompatible with good husbandry, the last hundred deer were now transferred to Richmond Park. At about the time of the royal wedding, the new Valley Gardens, with their amphitheatres of azaleas, were developed as a hillside complement to the waterside paths of the Savill grounds. These changes embodied a new chapter of local history for Royal Lodge. But the King knew he could no longer find time to write a personal history of his home, and Sir Owen Morshead at last helped him to finish the task by writing a private monograph.

The years were closing in. After his first operation in March 1949, the King returned to Royal Lodge, and for the first time since George IV a service of Communion was held in the house. Unable to walk more than a few paces, the King's inability to kneel to receive the Sacrament ran counter to his sense of proper conduct and he apologised repeatedly and was in great distress. But in his convalescence his ability to cut away the branches of an intrusive rhododendron ponticum was one of the symptoms of returning health. Then came his second, more serious operation for the removal of a lung — and again the joy of returning home to the Lodge. "As we drive through the gates we felt at once the calm of this place," he wrote to a friend. On February 1st 1952, he left Royal Lodge for the last time, to go to Sandringham.

11: THE FAMILY HOME

I

Every week, some nine months of the year, when her rota of royal duties concluded, Queen Elizabeth the Queen Mother unobtrusively left Clarence House for Royal Lodge. In the crystal triptych on her desk the typed sheet of engagements was fulfilled at last, and her glance of enquiry met only the lines of verse by Laurence Whistler engraved on the glass:

The crowds, the lights, the welcome… And (Sweet as them all) the going home!

In the car there was usually a dog, and there were always friends … so many friends in the pageant of hospitality that always filled and encircled the Queen Mother's private life. How many friends? Once, when a Lisa Sheridan photograph of her grandchildren at Royal Lodge especially charmed her, she ordered one hundred and ten copies: one for each individual, one for the married couples, one for family groups, so that we may at least double the figures in an estimate of close friendship … or treble them.

In the glasshouse reserved for melons, the Head Gardener may estimate the need of eight or ten for dinner. In the greenhouse the estimate of cut flowers for the house must not omit flowers in the guest rooms. All had been arranged with the steward by telephone from London, and the Queen Mother arrived at her country home to find the front door already open, her housekeeper, Mrs. Searles, waiting in welcome. In service at Royal Lodge since 1933, Mrs. Searles

183

was long known as "Campie" (for May Campbell) before she married Alfred Searles, the lodgekeeper, in the Royal Chapel.

There were always flowers in the entrance hall and the old rocking horses, too, flavoursome period pieces as they had become for adults, but mettlesome steeds still, to enchant younger grandchildren. The Queen Mother's bedroom, the decorative theme soft pink and blue, still opened from the ground floor corridor, to the left of the portico. A magnificent Banksian rose flourished against the private side wall just outside the windows; and fixed to a casement was the clock-like thermometer which King George VI invariably consulted every morning. In the octagon room, the King's desk had become the Queen Mother's own, never to be used by others, and always with letters awaiting her from friends and relatives who anticipated her homecoming.

One can picture, perhaps, a day in early spring, when a log fire has been banked up in the wrought-iron basket on the brick fireplace and the glow of the flames draws soft glints from the maple-panelled walls. The firelight warms the gilt bindings on the bookshelves and seems to draw smiles from the line of small oval-framed Georgian portraits that hang top to bottom like a pendant, a distinctive touch, near brocade-curtains beside the wide French window. Outside, on the broad terrace, the pinnacled box shrubs stand on rigid guard duty in their tubs and, beyond the lawn, the beckoning flowers of rhododendrons and azaleas draw one imperceptibly into the garden. Four maples glimmer in company with a weeping willow. Across the lawn the huge yellow clump of rhododendron luteum may have been planted by Colonel Gordon. The Queen Mother was well-informed on estate history, no one better. But appearances can be deceptive. The huge eucalyptus tree, towering more than fifty feet high, was planted in her own earliest years as chatelaine. A treasured glade of camellias, more than one hundred and fifty of differently named varieties, proved to be her husband's bequest to her of his last planting season.

Every corner, indeed, bears a memory, more sweet in remembrance than bitter. The Little House, less pristine than it used to be, awaits the housekeeping of Princess Margaret's daughter, little Lady Sarah, a family coincidence of name that reminds us of the Duchess Sarah, who so firmly founded the estate. The old nearby wire-mesh creosoted aviary has vanished, to be replaced by a sanctuary of more distinctive style, the imprint of Lord Snowdon who, one remembers, designed aviaries of greater fame than the one at Royal Lodge. In the dwarf formality of the Little House garden, the miniature sundial is firmly set in concrete, as it had to be when Prince Charles strenuously pushed it over as a boy of three, a feat since gleefully attempted by his brothers, Prince Andrew and Prince Edward. Then there are the two small and separate gardens which the "two little Princesses" once planted and assiduously filled. The Queen and her sister as children had their own tools and wheelbarrow, a little tool-house, and seats where a juvenile gardener could rest, her labour done, and presently the taskwork was handed down to Princess Anne. Neither the Queen nor Princess Margaret appeared to have inherited green fingers, but it was a long time before anyone dared disturb the first landscaping and architectural efforts of Charles, Prince of Wales in a garden patch he formed in infancy with a path of miniature bricks, and a bowl to serve as a tiny pool.

Each corner with its memories... Not far from the swimming pool is a bank formed from its excavated soil where the forsythias, pyracanthas and lilacs recall an afternoon of partnership when the King planted and his consort carried the shrubs to him like any husband and wife working together in the garden in a late autumn afternoon. In their early days on the Throne, when security somewhat excessively encircled the Lodge, it is said that the Queen Mother went walking in the rain and discovered a drenched policeman sheltering miserably under a tree. Sure enough, snug thatch-roofed hides were constructed, scarcely seen amidst the trees, to protect her guardians against the elements.

All gardens may feature gifts from friends, and this one more than others, with plants and shrubs untold whispering their sentiment. In a tub alone on the lawn in summer there stands a little myrtle tree, thick and bushy and nearly three feet high. It was grown from a sprig of myrtle that the Queen Mother carried in her wedding bouquet, and myrtle shrubs in other smaller tubs emulate this royal tradition, living trophies from the weddings of the two daughters of the house. In winter they are taken into the saloon or stand in the hall.

But shall we return to the house?

II

Among all the apartments, stuffy or spacious, large or small, in the world of royalty, the drawing-room — the saloon — of Royal Lodge is unique. Designed by Wyatville as a dining-hall of noble proportions, as we have seen, a banqueting chamber fit for a King, it had been restored in the Queen Mother's time to a drawing-room not of splendour — this is not the first effect — but of light and space. The five imposing sets of arched Gothic windows, each six feet or more in width, seem almost to heighten the full light of day. An autumn sunset burnishes the whole room with rose and gold; a gale seems enlarged, each great window tumultuously patterned with rain.

In its clear, unsullied light, the saloon is not, one thinks, the happiest room for a lady of middle-age, except a woman of unusual assurance and sincerity.

The paintwork, green and cool, is fresh but unflattering. The absence of any mirror may be more than accidental. The exacting light is softened only by the lofty ceiling, where panels of bossed and beaded plaster panels, high again nearly as the windows, seem to trap and tone the reflections from the terrace.

After nightfall, when the five pairs of heavy curtains are drawn and the lustres of the three great chandeliers glint and sparkle, the atmosphere is gaily theatrical; and then softened and different again at the touch of a switch, with only the golden glow of the wall sconces, the candelabra on the stone mantelshelf or the island pools of light of the table lamps. Now it becomes a room of enclosure and comfort, shadows melting against the soft green walls, a sense almost of religious sanctuary subtly evoked in the church-like silver-edged Gothic mouldings.

The room has changed little, save in mellowing, since the Queen Mother first furnished it when she was Duchess of York. Extending nearly the full length and breadth, the timeless Persian carpet, rose, blue and gold, is a little more scuffed: it has so often formed a dancefloor and so rarely suffered the indignity of being rolled up. Hearthside rugs are changed, none immune from wood sparks however well-chosen the logs in the wrought-iron grate. There are contrasts that only the life of a Queen can provide: a utilitarian rush log-basket set against an eighteenth-century pole-screen bearing the coat-of-arms of King George VI, a delicate French clock on the chimneypiece keeping company now with a tiny framed picture of St. Paul's Walden Bury, and yet again at the far end of the apartment the Chair of State of the Queen Mother's Coronation set against the arbours and hinds of a medieval tapestry. Near the fireplace a rosewood chest offers a marquetry of flowers in cool and engaging contrast to the flames and, nearby, a display table of bibelots enchant the eye from a cosy wing-chair.

Here, as in the garden, as in every home, remembrances fuse. Furniture may be moved, leaving barely an imprint, only to be missed and restored to its original status. When, in 1952, the Queen Mother found herself alone, in sad truth the Queen dowager, she was prepared for retirement, prepared even, in her humility of spirit, for the new Queen to take over the occupancy of Royal Lodge. In making it his private home, King George VI had also made it the Sovereign's private house, and so the tradition might well have been passed on. The new Queen, however, drew her mother away from these sombre possibilities. Princess Margaret moved into a downstairs room across the hall — perhaps her father's one-time study — in order to be constantly near her mother. At this time, the two desks still stood in the saloon and Princess Margaret worked at one while the Queen Mother used the other. The one concession to change was that the King disliked flowers on his desk, and now a crystal vase of flowers decked each worktop.

The two women found a new and close companionship. One may imagine how precious that communion became to the Queen Mother, and why she did not deter Princess Margaret during that ill-starred phase when Group Captain Peter Townsend came riding across the park from Adelaide Cottage. Happily, the impact of that episode has long since faded. A symbol of the close understanding and sympathy between mother and younger daughter was expressed when in tacit counterpoint to the tapestry and Coronation chair at the far end of the saloon, Princess Margaret arranged a table at the other end to harbour her own collection of miniature busts and statuettes of royal forbears and kinsfolk. The Princess loved this highly personal assemblage, each figure occupying its special and appointed place, and she knew at once if one of the fifty or sixty pieces had been moved. The story goes that the collection was transferred to Kensington Palace when Princess Margaret established her own married home there with Lord Snowdon, only to be returned to her mother's safekeeping when there seemed a risk of breakages from irrepressible and quick baby fingers.

With the coming of Mr. Antony Armstrong-Jones, the Queen Mother was quick to recognise her daughter's deepening interest and may have been the first to reflect on the prospects of her happiness. Many young men came to the Lodge through the years; they came singly or with accompanying young ladies, perhaps to tea, perhaps progressively to Saturday lunch and tea, and Mr. Armstrong-Jones was one of the few who at a surprisingly early stage came for the weekend. The names of some became familiar if only from the interminable matrimonial speculation in the newspapers. Others more fortunate were not subjected to the groundless incessant rumours.

At the time of the Townsend furore it was said that photographers trespassed into the Royal Lodge grounds in the hope of a quick photographic scoop with a telescopic lens, and the police had to probe every clump of shrubs before changing patrol. Things never again reached that pitch. It would appear that the public fervour was shamed. (One must add that if Melville and perhaps Ackermann had not trespassed to make their drawings in the days of George IV we should not now know what the first Royal Lodge looked like.) It is sometimes thought that Mr. Armstrong-Jones first went to Royal Lodge as a professional photographer, his mission a semi-professional one, that of photographic Princess Margaret for the set of pictures to be released on her twenty-ninth birthday. But in reality he was there as a friend, an accepted visitor who had discreetly known the social life of the Lodge, the dinner-parties and disc dances, the riding and walking with the dogs, the garden-chair sunning, the gaiety of the swimming pool and the fire-lit conversation of the octagon room, for many months.

III

As early as 1957 the uninhibited smile of the nine-year-old Prince Charles in an Armstrong-Jones photograph suggests the assurance of a small boy with a friend rather than a child facing a stranger's camera. As late as 1959, whenever Commander Colville, the Queen's press secretary, faced interrogation on Princess Margaret's future, he met the questions without twitching an eyelash towards the clue with which he had decked half the wall of his office, a huge blown-up picture of the royal children from an Armstrong-Jones negative. At the Lodge, the successful young photographer figured unobtrusively in the social flow of a group of Princess Margaret's friends that included Jocelyn Stevens, John Betjeman, Noël Coward, Lady Elizabeth Cavendish … representatives, as was once remarked, of publishing, poetry, the play and the peerage. So much treacled nonsense has been written of Lord Snowdon's career as a photographer that one is in danger of forgetting the family background, the beauty of Nymans, the respectability of Eaton Terrace, the spacious Georgian charm of his stepfather's home at Womersley Park, the maternal grand-uncle who had left a sliver of family wealth,

190

a million pounds, to the Royal Society, and the barrister father, Q.C., who had been a High Sheriff of Caernarvonshire despite the impediment of a "marriage dissolved."

Eton, Cambridge, and irreproachable connections were there, but so was audacity, independence ... and the incalculable streak that won the Queen Mother's quick, amused friendship. None of the other young men of Princess Margaret's acquaintance could claim a grandfather remotely like Tony's, a brain specialist and psychiatrist who had listed his recreation in Who's Who as "retrospective contemplation." None of the others lived in a Pimlico basement or possessed a Thameside hideaway at Wapping. Every phase of Tony's activities interested Princess Margaret and every facet of his bubbling sense of humour, his spontaneity, practical good sense and ingrained courtesy won appreciation from the Queen Mother. Apart from talent and vitality, the photographer of the subsequent news-clippings seems to have little in common with the engaging, sociable and yet solitary young man for whom the doors of Royal Lodge were ever more open.

Watching their dawning affection, aware that they were two of a kind before the young people knew it themselves, the Queen Mother contrived opportunities for them to enjoy one another's company, more and more, in the natural unfettered setting of her home. Royal Lodge has always enjoyed a quick scene-shifting informality: dinner on the terrace until the moths flutter against the candles in the summer dusk, tea under the old oak or, again, tea in the saloon on a winter day with the table drawn close to the fire. And there were quiet weekends when the Queen Mother arranged to be visiting elsewhere, and the young people had the house almost to themselves, and card tables were brought from the landscape room and laid for dinner so that the two might both eat and watch television, all the more entertaining for one another's companionship.

There were the dances, with the occasional chairs — the Queen Mother's set of lacy charmers of Sheraton "mock bamboo" style — arranged in conversational groups. The screen around the drink tray would be moved away, the radiogram pounded music and presently, with the mellowing atmosphere, a group would gather around the piano in the corner. Princess Margaret would sometimes spend hours at the keyboard beforehand, practising; and the Queen Mother and her daughter occasionally indulged in duets. Visiting Royal Lodge the Queen was often content to sit and listen, remembering the dutiful hours when she herself sat at the piano in the saloon, at her music lessons as a Princess.

The house became especially a family rendezvous on polo afternoons. Smith's Lawn, named after a Georgian park-keeper who first improved the sward with his sheep, lies barely a mile to the south and formed the setting of home matches for the Windsor Park team and the practice games of the Household Brigade polo club. Here the Queen would sit under the canvas marquee on a summer afternoon, simultaneously watching her horses in a televised race-meeting and the fluctuating excitement of each chukka. Queen Victoria would not have approved, for she considered polo cruel, for the ponies. Smith's Lawn, incidentally, formerly served as a light aircraft flying field for the Duke of York and Edward VIII, and paratroop displays have been staged here. It also afforded a quick helicopter take-off for Prince Philip and for the Queen Mother herself. Not all the modern journeys to Royal Lodge were made along the Great West Road.

Polo, racing, steeplechasing, future plans, family gossip, books, pictures, friends ... one need not hide under a couch as the Boy Jones did in Buckingham Palace to catch the easy swing of Lodge table-talk. Domestic affairs creep in, and even building problems still, as in the days when the youthful Duke and Duchess of York enjoyed their picnic meals in the empty saloon or waited for Willett's man amid the smell of paint and linseed oil. When you have a house, there is always something further to do, even for the Queen Mother's achievement of finished perfection. At one point, hairline cracks were noticed in her bedroom wing and the structure had to be underpinned after other remedies had failed. The nearby explosion of wartime bombs, it was suggested, may have disturbed more of the underground work that John Nash — and Mr. Dolby — scamped when building anew on the home of the Sandbys.

And there were later villains. To the Queen Mother's dismay and annoyance, symptoms of damp discoloured and stained her pristine exterior rose-pink paintwork above the saloon, creeping from beneath the lead-flats of the roof; and Mr. Menzies or some other Victorian architect must be adjudged guilty of failing to provide a damp-course within the roof-plinth.

Growing families, too, have altered the first-visualised requirements of the guest rooms. The staircase next to the octagon room used to lead up both to the guest suites and the accommodation that Mr. Havers, the steward, sometimes termed "the female staff rooms." Some of the latter evolved into nursery suites in the early days when the Queen and Prince Philip went on their first overseas tours. Later, the nursery rooms were primarily for the Snowdon family as the weekend adjunct to Kensington Palace. New generations of young cousins raced, voices shrilling, down the long glades; and if the Queen Mother's eyes grew wistful it was perhaps with the kindling thought of herself, and her younger brother as children, scampering with the same delight until they fell breathless in the new-mown grass. The memories of Royal Lodge have enfiladed half a lifetime of kinsfolk and close acquaintance. Other romantic attachments have developed in its setting, including marriages in the Queen Mother's household, as well as the love-match of Princess Margaret and Antony Armstrong-Jones. The sunken garden seems an enclosure created for confidences. It was doubtless in recognition of the part played by Royal Lodge in Princess Margaret's romance that the young couple had their betrothal photographs taken there. Early the following Sunday, a day or two after the announcement of their engagement, they went together to the Royal Chapel across the drive for Holy Communion, and it was to Royal Lodge that they returned immediately after their honeymoon. It is usually thought that Lord Snowdon chose his title in tribute to Caernarvon forefathers. It may be so. But Royal Lodge lies on the slopes of Snow Hill, or Snowdon as it was originally called in the earliest deeds.

When Princess Alexandra and Mr. Angus Ogilvy became engaged, the latter Princess characteristically chose her own mother's wedding anniversary for the announcement date. Yet Royal Lodge had proved part of the setting of their love story, also, and in fixing the date of their wedding day on April 24th, midway between the Queen's birthday and the Queen Mother's wedding anniversary, it may be that the mise-en-scène was accorded its due recognition.

It has often been said that the strength of the modern monarchy is in its precept as a family example, and the abiding private centre of this family felicity in our time has been Royal Lodge. It is a paradox that George IV, the most unhappily married of monarchs, should gaze from his canvas shadows in the place of honour above the chimneypiece. Long may the portrait remain, where it was hung by the former head of the house. But in the fullness and fidelity of time, let other sentiments prevail and let it be replaced, one suggests, by a more fitting portrait, perhaps of the lady who, more than any other woman, transformed Royal Lodge into a home, or perhaps of her partner, happiest of husbands and kindest of fathers, that noble and self-denying monarch, King George VI.

BIBLIOGRAPHY AND AUTHOR'S NOTE ON SOURCES

Any study of twentieth-century royalty must necessarily turn to two definitive sources, and I must particularly acknowledge my indebtedness to *King George VI* by Sir John Wheeler-Bennett (Macmillan) and *Queen Mary* by James Pope-Hennessy (Allen and Unwin). In turning to the past, the 1954 edition of the collected works of Thomas Love Peacock contains an essay 'The Last Day of Windsor Forest' which researchists appear to have ignored. I am also most grateful to Harold A. Albert for allowing me to refer to the manuscript of his forthcoming biography *Queen Victoria's Sister* (Hale).

Other works that I have found particularly helpful include:

Windsor Old and New — T. Eustace Harwood.

Round And About Windsor — Olwen Hedley.

The Court at Windsor — Christopher Hibbert.

A History of Windsor Forest — G. M. Hughes.

King Charles II — Arthur Bryant.

The Early Churchills — A. L. Rowse.

The Duchess Sarah — Mrs. Arthur Colville.

Letters of a Grandmother (Dss of Marlborough) — Thomas and Paul Sandby — Wm. Sandby, ed. G. S. Thomson.

William Augustus, Duke of Cumberland — Evan Charteris.

The Drawings of Paul and Thomas Sandby — A. P. Oppé.

The Daughters of George III — D. M. Stuart.

Portrait of the Prince Regent — D. M. Stuart.

Mary Frampton's Journal — ed. H. G. Mundy.

John Nash — John Summerson.

George the Fourth — Roger Fulford.

Royal Pavilion — Clifford Musgrave.

Memoirs of George the Fourth — Robert Huish.

Repository of Arts 1823 — Rudolph Ackermann.

The First Lady Wharncliffe — ed. Caroline Grosvenor.

The Life and Times of Queen Adelaide — Mary F. Sandars.

The Girlhood of Queen Victoria — ed. Viscount Esher.

Victoria R. I. — Elizabeth Longford.

The Letters of Queen Victoria — ed. A. C. Benson and Viscount Esher.

The Early Years of the Prince Consort — Charles Grey.

The Prince Consort — Roger Fulford.

The Prince Consort and His Brother — ed. Hector Bolitho.

The Queen Thanks Sir Howard — M. H. McClintock.

King Edward the Seventh — Philip Magnus.

Windsor Castle Furniture — Guy Lacking.

My Memories of Six Reigns — Princess Marie Louise.

King George V — John Gore.

A King's Story — The Duke of Windsor.

The Little Princesses — Marion Crawford.

Royal Gardens — Lanning Roper.

The Gardens in the Royal Park at Windsor — Lanning Roper.

The Royal Gardeners — W. E. Shewell-Cooper.

From Cabbages to Kings — Lisa Sheridan.

My Life with Princess Margaret — John Payne.

ACKNOWLEDGEMENTS

This book originated as an intended entertainment for a royal lady and may now, I hope, prove of wider public interest without too close an intrusion into private life. I was accorded research facilities into the Royal Lodge papers formerly with the Crown Estate office (crest 16, 1–22, etc.) and I have drawn much fresh material from the original estimates and letters of the architect, John Nash, as well as from the relevant papers of the Lord Chamberlain's department. Although cast over a wider terrain, my enquiries in some respects followed those of Sir Owen Morshead, Librarian Emeritus to the Queen; and as a lodestar late on my horizon I must express my sense of obligation to his monograph "George IV and Royal Lodge," which he first prepared for the private use of King George VI.

Alongside the Bibliography, I have to make it clear that, where otherwise unacknowledged, copyright is reserved in the quotations from royal journals and correspondence found in my narrative.

HELEN CATHCART

A NOTE TO THE READER

If you have enjoyed this book enough to leave a review on **Amazon** and **Goodreads**, then we would be truly grateful.
The Estate of Helen Cathcart

Sapere Books is an exciting new publisher of brilliant fiction and popular history.

To find out more about our latest releases and our monthly bargain books visit our website:
saperebooks.com